THE BIBLICAL DOCTRINE
OF MAN IN SOCIETY

ECUMENICAL BIBLICAL STUDIES No. 2

THE BIBLICAL DOCTRINE OF MAN IN SOCIETY

G. ERNEST WRIGHT

AND AN
ECUMENICAL COMMITTEE
IN CHICAGO

Published for the Study Department
World Council of Churches by

SCM PRESS LTD
56 BLOOMSBURY STREET
LONDON

First published March 1954
Second impression April 1956

Printed in Great Britain by
The Camelot Press Ltd., London and Southampton

CONTENTS

INTRODUCTION

IN JANUARY 1950, the writer was asked by the Study Department of the World Council of Churches to convene a group of biblical scholars from the various theological schools in the Chicago area, in order to initiate discussions leading toward the preparation of a document concerned with *The Biblical Doctrine of Man in Society*.

Over several years the Study Department had been engaged in a broad enquiry on 'The Social and Political Message of the Bible Today', the outcome of which was published in 1951 in a symposium entitled *Biblical Authority for Today*. It was decided to carry further this enquiry in the form of a series of monographs on particular themes. The biblical doctrines of Man in Society, Work and Justice were in the first place selected for exploration in an ecumenical setting, and different groups of scholars were invited to assume responsibility for each subject.

During 1950 and 1951 the Chicago group held a series of seven two-day conferences in which consultants from outside the biblical field of study participated. An outline for the presentation of the material was decided upon and repeatedly revised in the successive meetings. All of the members of the group, whose work permitted them to do so, prepared papers on various phases of the topic. These were read, discussed and revised. It was then left to the writer to draw up a document on the basis of these papers and their discussion. It was felt that a unified presentation from one perspective would be preferable to a symposium, or to a patchwork of material written from various perspectives. In these circumstances the writer obviously carries sole responsibility for the content of the document.

7

It must be emphasized however, that this monograph could not have been written in its present form without the help of the Chicago committee; and the names of those who participated are listed at the end of this Introduction. Not only were the preliminary papers and discussion important, but the members of the group also went over the first draft of the completed manuscript and made numerous suggestions for its correction and improvement. Particular mention must be made of a preliminary paper by Professor Willem F. Zuurdeeg, which formed the basis of Chapter I, Section B; of the paper by Professor J. Coert Rylaarsdam, the substance of which is contained in a shortened and revised form in Chapter II, Section A; of the paper by Professor Amos N. Wilder, which was adopted with little change as Section E in Chapter III; and of the paper by Professor Eugene S. Wehrli which was of considerable assistance in Chapter IV, Section D. Other papers were also used, even when not extensively quoted, particularly for background material; and a complete list of those prepared will be found appended. It should also be stated that a study conference on the topic was held in Göttingen, Germany in July, 1951. A selection of the preliminary papers of the Chicago group had been sent to this conference, which in turn sent us valuable comments about them.

The Chicago group had considerable difficulty at the outset with two words in the topic assigned to it. One was the word 'doctrine' and the other was the word 'society'. The first might suggest that the Bible contains a systematic teaching or dogma concerning man, community and their relationship. It can be interpreted to mean that dogma and the biblical revelation in a particular history are to be equated. Yet it was quite clear to us that the word 'doctrine' in this case must not be interpreted in such a manner. It is instead to be understood in the sense of 'testimony' and 'inferential teaching'. The biblical concern with a story of what has happened, inter-preted both with reference to God and to the revelation of God which it provides, does not of itself furnish us with, or exhibit a primary interest in, propositional dogmatics in systematic form. Hence the word 'doctrine' in the title of this monograph means, on the one hand, the Bible's *testimony* to what God has done, and, on the other hand, the *inferences* which the biblical writers have made from the testimony, and those which we believe we should make in the light of our own historical situation.

The difficulty encountered with the word 'society' lay in its extremely general nature. It is not a biblical word, and it is frequently used of all men, regardless of whether they possess anything in common other than their common humanity. On the other hand, it is also used of a group of people who are united by common interest, common heritage, and/or common organization. It is to be doubted that this monograph avoids the ambiguity which is inherent in the term. When used of 'the people of God' in the Bible, it is here considered to be synonymous with the terms 'community', 'church', the 'fellowship', etc.; and generally has the term 'new' or 'redeemed' appended to it. Yet it is also used for the national groupings of men outside the 'people of God'. This is clear when the plural is employed, as in the title of Chapter II; when the singular appears, it is synonymous with the term 'world' as used in the New Testament.

In our discussions of the topic one of the first problems which we faced, and one which did not cease to trouble us, was the question of the unity of the Bible and the manner in which the material should be presented. It was soon decided that in this study the Bible must be treated as a whole. Some form of unity is implied in the very term 'Bible' and in the doctrine of the canon. For this reason we could not treat the

Old and New Testaments separately, leaving it to our readers to put the data together. A purely historical or developmental approach, therefore, was felt to be inadequate; what was particularly needed was a comprehensive and synthetic treatment of the whole. Yet the unity of the Bible is not a static uniformity of all its parts. The primary area of unity lies in its historical testimony to, or proclamation of, God's activity (*kerygma*; see Chapter III, Section A); but the inferences and applications drawn from the testimony in particular historical situations may show considerable variation. In addition, a few books of the Bible, notably those containing the Wisdom literature of the Old Testament, exhibit scant interest in the historical testimony, or in the doctrine of the new society involved in it. These facts were taken by us to mean that it is impossible to treat any biblical theme without constant attention to biblical history and to variety in viewpoint and situation among the biblical writers. Yet in dealing with the topic assigned to us we were confronted with severe limitations of time and space. To give a synthetic treatment meant that it was impossible to present a complete history of each theme or to describe in detail the variations in emphasis and perspective. What we have tried to do is to present what we believe to be the dominant emphases of biblical literature, while dealing with change and variety only at those points where it is crucially important to do so.

Involved in the problem of unity is the problem of the relation between the Old and New Testaments. We approach the Scripture as members of the Christian community which acknowledges Christ as Lord. This means that our perspective is and must be Christocentric and that for us Christ is the Lord of the Scripture, including the Old Testament: that is, the unity of the Bible is to be found in him. Yet what precisely does this mean for biblical interpretation, and how does it govern our method of presenting the topic before us? In *Guiding Principles for the Interpretation of the Bible*, as set forth by the Wadham College study conference in 1949,[1] it was stated that in the attempt to discover the biblical teaching on a specific social or political problem we should begin with the teaching of the New Testament, in the light of which we should then turn to the Old Testament in order to view the problem in the perspective of God's total revelation. This method of presentation has been generally followed in the present monograph, except in specific cases where the historical approach seemed necessary and in the many instances where the attempt has been made to furnish generalizations summarizing the whole (e.g. in Chapters I and IV).

Nevertheless, to some readers the monograph may still appear deficient in Christological emphasis. One major difficulty in the construction of statements which attempt to summarize the teaching of the Bible as a whole on the doctrines of man and society is the fact that the Old Testament, as we now understand it, is not a book about Christ primarily, but about the activity of God which leads us to his act in Christ. Christ is thus the clue to the meaning of the Old Testament because he is the destination of, and thus the guide to, its contents, whereas at the same time the Old Testament, with its presentation of the living God, is the clue to Christ. For this reason the viewpoint which dominates the present monograph, and which is the clue to many generalizations that at first glance seem not to be Christocentric, is focused in the conception of God's redemptive activity, and of Christ as God's supreme act. Such a view

[1] This document has been printed in a number of different places: e.g. *The Ecumenical Review*, Vol. II, No. 1 (Autumn, 1949), pp. 83-6; A. Richardson and W. Schweitzer, eds., *Biblical Authority for Today* (London and Philadelphia, 1951), pp. 240-3.

makes it possible to avoid many of the ambiguities involved in the procedures usually associated with the 'Christological exegesis' of the Old Testament. Theological and exegetical questions are closely related and intertwined, but the relation of the Old Testament to the New is not clarified by Christomonism but by 'the full Trinitarian faith of the Church'.[1] This is not to say that the full Trinitarian faith is developed as doctrine in Scripture itself, but it does affirm that the living God through the Holy Spirit confronts us with his truth even in those pages of the Old Testament which in themselves say nothing about Christ and which are not always related even typologically to New Testament events. 'God is not confined; He speaks in his own way and by diverse methods; but He is the same God in both Testaments, the Lord of Israel and the Father of our Lord Jesus Christ.'[2]

Finally, in presenting this monograph we are aware of a number of its serious deficiencies. Among them is the question of the relevance of the data here discussed to the modern Christian and the modern Church. The chapters which follow are decidedly weak at this point. Yet we have understood that our task was biblical study and that we were not to trespass needlessly into other areas for which the World Council through its Study Department has inaugurated special inquiries. The monograph is thus offered as an introductory study in the hope that whatever of value it contains may prove useful in other ecumenical discussions. I am much indebted to Professor Holt Graham for preparing the Subject Index.

G. ERNEST WRIGHT

McCormick Theological Seminary
February 12, 1953

[1] *Ibid.*, Article I, Section (*e*).
[2] Cf. further the writer in A. Richardson and W. Schweitzer, eds., *Biblical Authority for Today*, pp. 226–9.

THE CHICAGO COMMITTEE

*and the Preliminary Papers
which it Prepared*

Professor Otto J. Baab, Garrett Biblical Institute, Evanston, Ill.

Professor Edward P. Blair, Garrett Biblical Institute, Evanston, Ill.

Professor Chalmer E. Faw, Bethany Biblical Seminary, Chicago, Ill.

Paper: 'Man as Social'

Professor Floyd V. Filson, McCormick Theological Seminary, Chicago, Ill.

Paper: 'Theological Presuppositions of the Biblical Doctrine of Man in Society'

Professor Holt Graham, Seabury-Western Theological Seminary, Evanston, Ill.

Paper: 'The Biblical View of the World'

Professor Paul E Keen, Evangelical Theological Seminary, Naperville, Ill.

Paper: 'The Divine Redeemer'

Professor Walter C. Klein, Seabury-Western Theological Seminary, Evanston, Ill.

Paper: 'The Relationship between the Redeemed Society and the World in the Spheres of Religion and Culture'

13

Professor Lester J. Kuyper, Western Theological Seminary, Holland, Mich.

Paper: 'Man as Creature'

Professor Julius R. Mantey, Northern Baptist Theological Seminary, Chicago, Ill.

Paper: 'The Divine Election'

Professor J. Coert Rylaarsdam, Federated Theological Faculty, University of Chicago

Paper: 'Man as Sinner'

Professor Don E. Smucker, Mennonite Biblical Seminary, Chicago, Ill.

Paper: 'The Task of the Redeemed Society'

Professor Eugene S. Wehrli, Elmhurst College, Elmhurst, Ill.

Paper: 'The Relationship between the Redeemed Society and the World in Political Life'

Professor Amos N. Wilder, Federated Theological Faculties, University of Chicago

Paper: 'Individual and Community in the New Age'

Professor C. Umhau Wolf, Chicago Lutheran Theological Seminary, Maywood, Ill.

Paper: 'The Nature and Scope of the Redeemed Society'

Professor G. Ernest Wright, McCormick Theological Seminary, Chicago, Ill.

Paper: 'The Community Life of the New Society'

CONSULTANTS

Professor James Luther Adams, Federated Theological
Faculties, University of Chicago
   Paper: 'Man in Community as Seen by Modern Socio-
   logy'

Professor James Hastings Nichols, Jr., Federated Theological
Faculties, University of Chicago
   Paper: 'The Responsible Society in the Perspective of
   Church History'

Professor Willem F. Zuurdeeg, McCormick Theological
Seminary, Chicago, Ill.
   Paper: 'The Redeemed Society in Economic Life'

I

INDIVIDUAL AND COMMUNITY IN THE BIBLE

In the non-Christian world a characterizing feature of much of the sacred literature is teaching on a variety of spiritual, moral and ritualistic matters. By contrast, the Christian Bible has as its chief concern the confessional recital of a particular history as revealing both the true nature and purpose of God and his sovereignty over all history. The man of the world desires from his religion particular directions as to how best he may live and achieve security in society and in the cosmos as they exist; and this teaching his religious literature provides. By contrast, the Bible offers him, first of all, a proclamation of what God has done in history, whence a knowledge of God's future intention is gained. Accompanying the proclamation is a challenge for man to commit himself, to accept a calling in the historical scene, and to become a member of a social organism which God himself has brought into being and which now exists under the Lordship of Jesus Christ. Through his action in history, God is known to be engaged in a dramatic struggle with the powers which are responsible for this world's darkness. He has decreed the death of the gods (e.g. Ps. 82), the annihilation of the powers of darkness, and the establishment of the new heavens and the new earth which shall be his eternal kingdom. In the accomplishment of this purpose he has chosen to serve as his mediate agent a people who in their weakness shall by his power confound the wisdom and strength of the world. The acts, the purpose and the demands of the Lord of history, together with the nature, task and life of the new community which he has brought into being as a foretaste of society's goal—these constitute the Bible's central content to which all its teachings are subsidiary.

It is thus clear that what is primary in the religious literature of mankind is in the Bible of secondary concern, vitally important, to be sure, but nevertheless set within the framework of the central proclamation. It is equally clear that, while the chief purpose of other sacred literature is scarcely to bear testimony to the community which has been created, it is precisely from biblical faith that the Church has come into existence and it is the biblical proclamation which continues to direct, sustain and constrain the Church's life and inner being. At the Bible's centre, therefore, is a Power who has purposed to create and sustain community, a community which is to exist in love and in peace, united in common allegiance to its Lord. The first fruits of this Divine purpose are to be seen in many historical evidences, though the hope and trust which God himself has created leads the eye of faith beyond past and present to the future consummation of true community throughout the whole creation.

This being so, we comprehend the centrality of the biblical concern with community. Indeed, it is to the people of God, Israel and the Church, that the Bible gives its primary attention, rather than to individuals as such. What to us and to most of the world's religions should be the dominant concern—namely, the life of the individual in his world—is in the Bible relegated to an important but nevertheless secondary position. God has brought into being, through redemptive acts which have culminated in Christ, a community in which each individual is called to participate. Individual and community are held together in a viable relationship without either being lost in concentration upon the other. Yet the formation of the community is God's central act; to it he has revealed its election, its task and its goal. The individual finds his true life when he possesses a calling within the community, when his election is understood to fulfil a portion of the community election, when in complete loyalty to the Lord who binds all diversity into unity he discovers the time of his life to be over-arched by the time of the new community, which in turn is transcended by the redemptive purpose, the 'eternity' of God.

This aspect of biblical faith is difficult for the modern Church either to comprehend or to appropriate because of its involvement in cultures which have rootage in a diversity of soils. The ecumenical Church has become increasingly and painfully aware that it does not possess that knowledge of the gospel and of its implications for the individual, social and political life of our time which will enable it to speak with confidence either to itself or to the world. This awareness has a range and depth which make it a new thing in the Christian scene. It is born of the judgment of God, made clear to us in the spiritual and political confusion of our century, in a civilization which has led, not to well-being, but to international turmoil and conflict. Hence we now see what formerly was largely hidden behind our semi-pagan hopes: namely that our civilization cannot be called Christian, nor can we longer identify Christianity with the political and social forms which we now seem capable of producing. In our uncertainty we are turning with renewed earnestness to the Gospel, but our progress is impeded because our luggage is heavy and not primarily biblical. Much of this luggage we are forced to carry simply because we live in the twentieth century. It is impossible easily to go back to the Bible and then return to our own life under the assumption that it provides all the equipment necessary, while forgetting that we cannot carry it all because of our previous load and that in any case it was never intended to supply us with many things we desire of it. Yet this much is certain: we must permit the Bible to make clear to us just what we are carrying and to impel us to choose between luggage. We cannot with indiscriminate taste carry everything which our hands touch or which we have inherited.

A. MODERN INDIVIDUALISM AND THE BIBLE

One article to which since the Renaissance we have clung with astonishing tenacity is a humanistic notion of the individual. With single-minded intensity the Western world has concentrated upon man the individual, upon his value, his worth, his rights, and his freedom, with the result that the sense of the meaning and purpose of community has been evaporating. This has happened so rapidly as to cause a vacuum which has been and is being filled by extreme and radical means. Society has been *atomized*, with the result that for the first time we hear of *mass man* in the industrial economy of our age. Man's lostness results in part from his loss of community, and from the conflicting attempts to interpret him. Liberal democracy has concentrated its attention upon that order of affairs which will assure the individual his maximum right and freedom as his greatest good, but to a large extent it has failed thus far so to intrepret the meaning of his social existence as to inspire his energies to goals beyond his immediate self-interest. A chaotic emptiness has thus come into existence, stabilized on the one hand by great industrial power and a frantic search for the meaning of the democratic tradition, and on the other by a variety of social and political programmes, the more extreme of which view man the individual as an unimportant segment of mass-man who for his own good must be directed or pushed toward the goal determined by the state or the élite within it.

Even the churches have so reflected our modern preoccupation with individual man that no matter how high the doctrine of the church to which a particular confession may adhere, in actual practice its congregations are a gathering of individuals who know little of Christian community in the biblical sense and expect little from it. Like secular clubs they meet in their various groups to hear speakers on a variety of topics which are usually unrelated, undigested and unillumined by the Christian faith. The Church's theology, traditionally so triumphantly and vigorously theocentric, tends now to be dominated by anthropology, by volume after volume like this one, on the nature of man and the bases of his social thought and action. The worship of the Church has been heavily influenced by individualistic pietism, concerned largely, not with the social organism, but with the individual's need of peace, rest and joy in the midst of the storms and billows of life. The self-centredness of the pietistic search for salvation tends to exclude vigorous concern with community. Hence, the modern Christian searches his Bible in a manner not unlike the pagan's study of his sacred literature, the purpose being to find inspirational, devotional and moral enlightenment for personal living, and nothing more. The sectarianism of the Churches, and their racial and national cleavages, are further expression of an individualism which distorts the nature of Christian society and provides excuse for the world's individualism.

Because of the Church's involvement in the egocentric predicament of modern culture, it is small wonder that the biblical conception of man in society has not been widely understood. Instead the tendency of nineteenth-century scholarship was to make the Bible speak in support of our concentration upon the individual. The significance of the Bible as a whole, it has been felt, lies in the gradual unfolding of ideals and values in its evolving historical process. Among these values is the emergence of the individual as an independent, responsive and responsible being; hence the Bible portrays the development of the ideal individualism. In the earlier stages of the history, it has been said, man the individual scarcely existed as a meaningful entity because he was submerged within his clan and tribe. The latter alone had meaning, and apart from them man was a lost soul, like Cain a fugitive and wanderer in the earth, upon whom society placed no value. This is the reason the nation as a whole occupied the centre of attention. To the community the law was addressed, the prophets were sent, and guilt was assessed. The whole tribe bore the guilt and assumed the consequence of individual lawlessness (e.g. Josh. 7; Judg. 19–21; II Sam. 21). Gradually, however, in the buffetings of history this tribal ethic broke down and true value emerged when the individual was liberated so that he possessed before God an independent status. Some New Testament scholars have been inclined to the view that it was Jesus who first 'discovered the individual'.[1] Old Testament scholars, on the other hand, have maintained that the discovery came earlier with the break-up of the Judean state, especially in Jeremiah and Ezekiel. An extreme statement of the view commonly accepted by the past three generations is the following:

'The traditional belief in Israel was that the human unit in religion was the nation; God was concerned with His people as a nation, and cared for the individual, if at all, only through his membership of the group. The covenant at the

[1] So, e.g. recently E. F. Scott, *Man and Society in the New Testament*, New York, 1946, p. 77.

22

Exodus had been made between the nation and God; the individual had no direct responsibility for his conduct to God; it was the concern of the nation as a whole to keep free from sin by observing the covenant. This idea of corporate personality in religion meant that if other individuals or the nation sinned, all, even the innocent, would be punished indiscriminately; and conversely that each Israelite had no individual moral responsibility to God, with whom in fact there could be no personal relation (cf. Jer. 31.29). *But Jeremiah from his own experience knew that the essence of religion was personal relationship between God and the individual.*'[1]

The last sentence betrays a major presupposition behind this viewpoint which alone has made it possible. So convinced have we been of the true nature of all 'high' religion as consisting chiefly in a dialogue between God and individual man that, since the Bible contains 'high' religion, we must surely find true individualism there and we are permitted to interpret biblical data in such a way as to demonstrate its existence.

The question, however, is whether our humanistic conception of true religion as consisting of a pure individualism is either valid in itself or a proper clue to the unlocking of the Bible. It is increasingly believed by the Church's biblical scholars today that the nineteenth-century views on this issue have not only misunderstood the Bible but have radically distorted it. On the one hand, it is important to realize that by the time Israel appeared on the scene of history, 'primitive' man, with his weakly developed consciousness of himself as a responsible person, as an 'I', had largely disappeared from the

[1] B. M. Pickering, 'Jeremiah', *A New Commentary on Holy Scripture*, ed. by Charles Gore, H. L. Goudge and Alfred Guillaume, New York, 1928, pp. 487–8. Italics are not in the original.

civilized world. The primitive conceptions of collective guilt may still be seen, but only as traces or relics surviving from a distant past. Ancient law clearly reveals the importance of individual responsibility when guilt and penalty were assigned by a court of law. In Israel's earliest collection of laws, the Book of the Covenant (Ex. 20–23), no less than in the pagan codes of an earlier date, collective retribution as a legal penalty has ceased to exist. To be sure, primitive notions survive among many of the people, and on isolated occasions the conception of the solidarity of guilt issued in drastic actions of collective retribution, as was the case with the sons of Saul (II Sam. 21). Yet such actions were outside the law; the latter did everything it could, as, for example, in the institution of cities of refuge, to limit blood revenge and collective retribution. Each individual was considered a subject at law and morally responsible for his actions.

On the other hand, we encounter in the Bible a religious basis for human responsibility radically different from anything found elsewhere. The result is a conception of personal responsibility to a single divine will, a responsibility which was without qualification or condition, which rested on the necessity of a complete and undeviating loyalty to the Lord who had brought a people into being by saving acts, and which arose not from legal necessity but from personal commitment. The characteristic address of God to his people was to be found in his 'Thou shalt', an apodictic type of legal address, which could only appear in a particular covenant relationship where God was known as the one personal Lord to whom alone belong all rights of sovereignty. In particular, it probably originated in cultic life, in solemn festivals sealing and renewing the covenant relationship (cf. Ex. 24; Deut. 27; Josh. 24). But this peculiar and characteristic feature of Israelite law promptly invaded the religiously

24

neutral law of civil community. The latter was borrowed very largely from contemporary society; yet in Israel it became a part of God's 'Thou shalt,' with the result that violation of law became more than a violation of civil community. It was a violation of the covenant and a personal affront to the Lord of the covenant.[1] Hence the sense of sin received a deeper dimension than was known elsewhere. It consisted in a betrayal of personal commitment which involved both rebellion against the Lord and violation of community. Hence also a sense of joy and exaltation in obedience, in the doing of God's will, could exist, one which was completely without precedent, for to most men religious exaltation appeared elsewhere than in service and vocation.

It is important to observe that the Law of Israel was interpreted as God's gracious gift to the nation which he had formed. A people who had been forced to live without the protection of law in Egypt were now given it and with it the promise of blessing. The law was understood as the revealed order for the called society. By its means and by the loyal devotion to its giver, of which it was the outward expression, Israel was to find the abundant life. It thus expressed God's gracious will for the community. Yet as community law it was by no means a tribal ethic. It transcended the limitations of such primitivism and formed the basis of a *new society* which in both popular and prophetic eschatology was seen as the first fruit of the universal Kingdom of God. Yet the individual was not lost or submerged in this community order. In it God's '*Thou shalt*' was characteristically singular, addressed to each individual. God's Word in the law singled out each person, so that as a responsible 'I' the individual heard the

[1] Cf. Walther Eichrodt, *Man in the Old Testament*, tr. K. and R. Gregor Smith; London and Chicago 1951, Chap. I; A. Alt, *Die Ursprünge des israelitischen Rechts*, Leipzig, 1934.

Word to the nation as being addressed to him personally. Man was not an insignificant and unsegregated component of a tribal mass. There was no such thing as 'mass society' in which the individual had no knowledge of himself, or of responsible selfhood, or of direct access to the sovereign power whose authority was absolute. In the covenant with the nation God dignified each member with his personal address, so that each one understood the responsible nature of his relationship to the Divine Person. The Lord of the nation was also the Lord of each of its individuals. Hence the powerful were warned to treat the weak with individual consideration, for the poor man had the right of direct access to God ('it shall come to pass, when he crieth unto me, that I will hear; for I am gracious,' Ex. 22.27).[1]

While the above indicates the core of the biblical conception of man in society, it is clear that there are different levels of emphasis in the various historical periods. The greatest danger to Israel was that of the transformation of the sacred covenant community into a state, with borrowed form of government and with increasing tendency toward secularization and accommodation. What relation had the state to the

[1] In this light we are able to comprehend the otherwise bewildering alternation between the plural and singular forms of address in the law (between 'ye' and 'thou'). Both community and individual are constantly in mind. The primary form in the apodictic law was the singular, even as it was in the secular casuistic law both in Israel and in the contemporary world. Yet the very nature of the Biblical conception of individual and community inevitably introduced the plural beside the singular, particularly in apodictic formulations and in hortatory exposition. For this reason the attempt by some to separate two different literary sources in Deuteronomy, characterized by 'ye' and 'thou' respectively, appears the height of futility (e.g. Carl Steuernagel, *Deuteronomium und Josua*, Göttingen, 1900). The constant back-and-forth movement between individual and community is a characterisitic of biblical literature: cf. e.g. Pss. 103, 130, 137.

divinely willed community as revealed in the law? Were the two identical, or did a tension exist between them? The prophetic attack upon the monarchy, and upon the chief buttresses of the state in priesthood and prophetic guilds, called upon the individual to 'turn', which meant a conscious decision on his part against the collective will and against his integration in the life of the community as it existed. The implications of the individual and community relationship in the covenant were then made clear in a new way. State and divine kingdom were not the same, and against the former the individual was called to take his stand. What, then, *was* the community in which and for which God wished him to fulfil his election? It was the true Israel which did not yet exist in organized form but which God through his acts of judgment was bringing into being. Meanwhile, the prophet and those touched by him experienced a sense of loneliness and of isolation, because it seemed that God had torn them from their social mooring. This is the explanation for the 'individualism' of Jeremiah and Ezekiel, and with the destruction of the Judean state it became the major problem of all surviving members of the former community. Hence the 'individualism' of the Exilic and Post-Exilic periods from the point of view of those then living was no happy achievement in freedom from former mass society. It was grounded in a new responsibility placed before the individual member of the people of God when the security of the political order was taken away; but its lonely isolation would soon be left behind in the true society which God was about to form.

When the Church in its study of the New Testament comprehends this situation in Israel as the divine preparation for the Body of Christ, it will be better prepared to comprehend the meaning of Christ's 'individualism'. While to be sure Jesus came into a complex world, heavily influenced by Greek culture and ideology, the New Covenant does not have its rootage in Hellenism. It is increasingly understood that the influence of Greek philosophy and the Hellenistic mystery cults upon the New Testament is at those points which are the least significant. The acts and teachings of Christ, far from 'discovering the individual' for the first time, were actually for the purpose of clearing the way of entrance into the new community, ordained of old and ardently awaited. The 'Sermon on the Mount' is firmly rooted in the apodictic tradition of Israel. Its prescriptions, like God's 'Thou shalt' of old, were addressed chiefly to the individual. Yet the attention is focused, not on the individual in and for himself alone, but on the manner of the Kingdom, for the time was at hand, the Kingdom in course of fulfilment, and individual decision and commitment were required. Man as man finds himself confronted with a choice, but awaiting him is the new community, the firstfruits of that which shall be. In other words, the relationship of individual and community in the New Testament is in essential aspects precisely that which existed in Israel.[1] The critical problem was the relationship between the called individual in the new community and the world in which both existed. While the individual is called forth from older social groupings into the elect society, he is not plucked out of the world but must live in it. Similarly, the new society exists in the midst of the old and is called to assume responsibility for it (see Chap. IV). Yet the world continually invades the Church and weakens its mission, even as it did in Israel.

It may thus be maintained that in the Bible we possess, not a description of the development of true individualism after

[1] The *composition* of the new community was radically changed, of course, because of the new answer given to the question, 'What is the true Israel?' Yet this difference was not clearly apparent until after Jesus' death.

28

the pattern of modern humanism, but instead the portrayal of the true relationship between individual and community, in which the true nature of both is revealed. Furthermore, the Bible also reveals the nature of our chief problem: life under the divine call and revelation in a world for which we are responsible, a world whose principalities and powers continually invade and threaten to overwhelm us, not alone by outward attack but especially by the more subtle interior and silent working, which ends in blinding our eyes and weakening our commitment.

B. RIVAL VIEWS OF THE NATURE OF THE WORLD

Still other conceptions which must be discarded if we are to understand the meaning and relevance of the biblical view of the relationship between man and community are non-biblical views regarding the nature of the cosmos and of human society within it.

In the Bible we are informed of certain basic orders of creation: God in relation to the universe, man in relation to God and to the earthly creation, and man in relation to the family. Otherwise the racial, social and political organizations of men on earth are conceived to have evolved after the 'fall'; they exist in and constitute the 'nations', the 'peoples', or the 'world' (see Chap. II). The new society has come to man's knowledge as a *revealed* order, one which God himself has made known to a people he has redeemed and to which all peoples shall one day belong, having left the old to enter into the new.

In the contemporary world of that time, as also in our own, the rival views were quite different. To the Egyptian the cosmos and human society within it were the eternal and unchanging 'givens' which no one can question. Society was a part of the order of creation. Both it and the cosmos were ruled by *ma'at*, 'the cosmic force of harmony, order, stability, and security, coming down from the first creation as the organizing quality of created phenomena and reaffirmed at the accession of each god-king. . . . If we render it "order" it was the order of created things, physical and spiritual, established at the beginning and valid for all time.' It both confirmed and established the *status quo*, from which no important deviations were considered a good.[1]

To the Mesopotamian, life was much more uncertain and unstable. The cosmic order was not a given; it was rather an achievement in the continual integration of many divine wills. It was an order of wills, a society, a state, which was not static but dynamic. Man, like the slave in the human city-state, had no share in the government of this cosmic society. He was created a slave to do the menial work of the earth, and his good life consisted in the obedience to hierarchical authority which befits the lot of a slave. His society was thus not a part of the order of creation, nor was it an order of revelation. The gods provided him a king to bring social order into existence and to insure its preservation. While the king ruled as an extension of the cosmic authority, the society for which he was responsible was largely a human contrivance, filled with difficulty and uncertainty.[2]

[1] John A. Wilson, *The Burden of Egypt*, Chicago, 1951, p. 48.

[2] Cf. Thorkild Jacobsen, *The Intellectual Adventure of Ancient Man*, ed. by H. and H. A. Frankfort *et al.*, Chicago, 1946, Chaps. V–VII. The relief on the Code of Hammurabi (*ca.* 1700 B.C.) has frequently been interpreted as a *revelation* of the law by Shamash, Lord Order, to the king. The contents of the Code make clear, however, that the king is merely being *commissioned* by the god to prepare the Code. Consequently, the king can speak of the law as 'my words', 'my justice', 'the law of the land which I enacted, the ordinances of the land which I prescribed' (cf. T. J. Meek, *Ancient Near Eastern Texts*, ed. James B. Pritchard, Princeton, 1950, pp. 163ff.). No Israelite king could ever make such a claim.

Of much more importance in its influence upon the Western civilization is the Greek conception of the world, as found in the work of the philosophers. To them the world is a well-ordered and harmonious whole, beautiful, good and rational. This order is eternal, without beginning or end, one which is uncreated by a god or gods. While the outward appearances of the world are confusion, change, decay and death, in its essential aspects it is an immutable structure, possessing power to arrange the particular into the whole and to act as an imminent norm by which all irrationality and disorder are to be judged. Man participates in this essential order because in himself he a micro-cosmos, possessing the same contrast between the changing and the changeless, between disorder and rational order, between body and mind, the physical and the spiritual.

This Greek viewpoint has its analogies to the Egyptian, for the essential structure of the world possesses divine rank and is eternal, without change. By contrast, the Bible proclaims the world as God's creation, limited in time, perishable in its present form and not eternal. It is a world alienated from God at the present time, under the power of sin and death, both the theatre and the object of God's redemptive action. It is the scene of conflict, objectified as a warfare between God and the nations and even his own people, between God and Satan, Christ and the Anti-Christ. This is the theme of history and will remain so until the final redemption, when the transformation will come.

In Western civilization, however, there is scarcely a more influential concept than that of the Greeks. Throughout the Middle Ages and the Reformation the biblical convictions were accepted largely as self-evident, but beginning in the seventeenth century and continuing to the present time the attempt has been made for the first time in Christian history to organize society on a completely non-religious basis. The programme of the enlightenment called for a neutral, secular society, in which there was no such thing as the 'holy'. Left-wing Protestants, especially among the Puritans, retreated from the position of the Reformation and the Medieval Church by drawing a line between the sphere of nature and that of grace. The latter had to do with personal and family worship; to the former belong the realms of politics, science and economics. In actual practice this separation has meant that in practical affairs we turn, not to the Bible which is without relevance except for personal life and certain ethical norms, but to the natural reason, as expressed in the social sciences, for our guidance. Paul Tillich speaks of this period as characterized by autonomy and heteronomy, in contrast to the former theonomous age.[1] Secular and humanistic norms are used for decision (autonomy), invaded occasionally by the attempt to impose other norms by a group or groups which may have the power to do so (heteronomy). The religious norms are, however, external, no longer accepted by the majority of the people; they constitute nothing but a 'decorative' theonomy.

In this separation of the spheres of grace and natural law, it has been a simple matter, even for Christians, to arrive unwittingly at the point where the Greek conception of the cosmos appears *self-evident*. The most important political ideas of Western man are convictions which find their ultimate rootage in the Greek world-view. If Western man believes that both the world at large and the individual are essentially a reasonable, moral and eternal order, then he is led to assume that man's social life also is essentially this rational structure. Though there are large sections of the world in which this

[1] Paul J. Tillich, *The Protestant Era*, Chicago, 1948; 'The World Situation', *The Christian Answer*, ed. by H. P. Van Dusen, New York, 1945, Chap. I.

view is not shared, it nevertheless is unquestioned by the great majority in the West. Certain examples of political convictions rooted in this world-view are as follows:

1. *Laissez-faire* Capitalism has held that because the world at large and human society in particular are essentially a harmonious, rational structure, all elements of disorder are accidental. This immanent structure is sufficiently powerful to correct all irregularity by its wholesome, healing process. Because this basic structure of society is essentially identical with that of the cosmos and with that of each individual, ultimate harmony is guaranteed only if the individual is given complete, unhampered freedom. All intentional interference is both immoral and destructive.

2. Marxism begins in the same manner and views the disorder of society as sin against the eternal, rational and harmonious structure of the cosmos. The chief form which the sin takes is that of yielding to the interests of specific social classes, but man, who is rational by essential inner structure, can do away with disorder and disharmony. Those in whom this rational and moral power is strongest can unite and lead mankind to the final revolution in which the sin against the eternal structure will be destroyed. Gradually a 'new man' will grow up who will establish the 'new society', both of which will be good. The absence of disorderly elements will make possible the harmonious community, without the harmony being established by institutions of coercion.

3. Democracy, too, believes in the rational structure of the individual, human society and the world. Hence it is possible to do something about those elements in society which are both causes and effects of disorder. Utopian democrats believe in the *essential* rationality of the cosmos and hold that it is possible to do away with disorder completely, so that an entirely harmonious society can be established. This utopia

by human, rational effort has frequently been confused with the Kingdom of God by sincere Christians who fail to realize its non-biblical rootage. Moderate democrats, on the other hand, do not hope to do away with disorder completely, because the world, society and man are rational to a certain extent only. In so far as the latter are rational, however, it is possible and necessary to lessen the power of disorderly institutions and trends in such a way as to make a secure life possible, even though the society does not achieve utopia.

It is impossible for the Christian Church to proclaim the biblical convictions about this world under God and to adhere at the same time with unquestioning equanimity to Graeco-Egyptian conceptions as they find expression in modern politics. All contemporary beliefs which tend in any way to deify elements of creation can only be denounced as idolatries. These include the belief in the essential harmonious order believed to be the divine core of the world, society and man (*laissez-faire* Capitalism, Marxism and utopian Democracy), and as well all tendencies to elevate to divine rank a specific race, a specific nation, or a specific class. Only with moderate democracy can the biblical convictions about the cosmos and human society be in any measure combined or accommodated, and then always with qualification. Yet because of the invasion of the Church by the world Christians have by no means been clear in their witness. Instead, they have betrayed their utter confusion, and, while denouncing the more overt forms of modern immorality, they have been overcome by the more basic paganisms, especially those that appear in idealistic dress and seem to promise salvation.

These, then, are some of the factors in our modern situation which hinder the Christian perception of the Biblical view of man in society, or even when perceived make difficult our comprehension of its relevant meaning.

34

II

MAN AND HIS SOCIETIES
IN THE WORLD

THE biblical viewpoint toward man and the world is conditioned by the knowledge of a profound and abnormal
disorder which exists within both. So pervasive is this disorder that not only is true life and a just society not to be found
among the kingdoms of this earth, but the beneficence of an
orderly nature is likewise disturbed. In the ancient polytheisms
the chief aim of worship was so to integrate man within his
society and society within nature that the whole would be
borne along in a cosmic and gentle rhythm. Biblical man had
no such confidence in the eternity of either society or nature.
The world in all of its aspects is a 'fallen' world, and the whole
of creation is in desperate need of redemption. Such orderliness
as nature possesses is due to a divine covenant with mankind
(Gen. 9), but there is no core or basic substance in the world
that possesses the permanency or stability of divine rank.
Nature is under a curse for man's sake (Gen. 3.17–19); sin is
joined to death which 'has gone abroad to all men' (Rom.
5.12); and creation by Divine sentence has become subject to
futility (Rom. 8.20).

Such a conception of the world is hardly self-evident; if it
were, one would expect to find it a common possession of
many peoples. The sense of security in society and nature
which is the aim of natural religion both to gain and sustain is

35

here sacrificed entirely. Its place is taken by the conception of a calling which involves a cross in the world and by the hope which sees meaning and fulfilment in history beyond the existing disorder because the Lord of history has been revealed both as Creator and Redeemer. In other words, the biblical view of the world and man was possible only because biblical man with his conception of the new society and the kingdom of God had it revealed to him. Israel was lost in Egyptian slavery until God appeared as Saviour; at the same time and later God's appearance as Judge revealed the nature of sin. For the Christian the act of God in Christ reveals at once the true nature of man in contrast to his actual state. The crucifixion shows the depth of this world's evil and the demonic powers to which all is subjected (I Cor. 2.8). Hence it is clear that the biblical knowledge of God, inferentially derived from what he had done and from the interpretative Word which accompanied his acts, carried with it a knowledge of the world as alienated from God, thus not existing in accordance with God's purpose in creation. For this reason, no ultimate loyalties or securities are to be sought in either society or nature as they now exist. For the same reason, man and his societies on earth are filled with disorder from which vain methods are sought as ways of release.[1]

A. Man as Sinner

According to the Bible, the problem of man and his society in the world, and the problem of the world itself, is that of man the sinner. When the Bible speaks about man, it speaks

[1] For example, the deification of rulers (Ezek. 28.2), the worship of creature rather than Creator (Isa. 41.5–7, 21–24, 46; Rom. 1.25); magic (Isa. 47.12–15); wisdom (Isa. 29.14; Jer. 18.18; I Cor. 1.18–2.9); material treasures (Luke 12.13–21), etc.

about a sinner whose existence stands in opposition to his origin. He is not the 'good' creature God created, for his 'existence-in-opposition'[1] openly manifests itself in the particular acts of his life. That this is true is an aspect of God's revelation in history. The biblical assumption of a 'fall' of man is based upon the realization of the utter difference between man as he now exists in and with his society and the willed purpose of God made known in redemptive acts. Hence biblical man could only assume that something had happened between creation and civilization, between the 'first man' and the emergence of the society and culture in which he now lives.

Yet this conception of man's 'fall' from grace involves a paradoxical assertion of man's impotence in depravity ('the imagination of man's heart is evil from his youth,' Gen. 8.21) and his capacity for responsibility ('Thou shalt worship the Lord thy God, and him only shalt thou serve,' Matt. 4.10; Deut. 6.13). This paradox arose from the honest effort to come to terms with the facts of human experience: man's actual existence and the inescapable demand placed upon him, his impotence and his creativity, his bondage and his freedom. Both are involved in the Bible's testimony about the meaning of life under God, and they are prevented from dissolving either into fatalism or moral optimism because they are bound together in a theocentric existence wherein God is acknowledged as free, sovereign and redemptive.

Christian theology traditionally has treated the doctrine of man under the following headings, derived chiefly from Gen. 1–11 and the Pauline letters: (1) man in the image of God, his nobility and worth; (2) the nature of man as a 'fallen' creature,

[1] Emil Brunner in *The Christian Understanding of Man* (*Church, Community and State*, Vol. 2, Oxford Conference Series, London, 1938), p. 162.

inheriting a capacity for sin from Adam; and (3) the atoning work of God in Christ. Yet in treating the subject in this way the tendency has been to focus attention upon man's inner nature, upon his faculties and capacities, upon his substantial being, as though he were an independent, self-dependent object of rational analysis. The result is an 'anthropocentricity which is the madness of modern theology,'[1] and which assumes a knowledge of man apart from a knowledge of man-in-relation-to-the-living-God. Brunner reminds us that the failure of 'orthodox theology' is that it turns man's 'actual existence' in this sense into a 'substantial deformity'. To do so removes God from the scene, as it were; and theology can become preoccupied with man as a problem in himself. Our attention is turned from vital and responsible self-understanding and decision before God's visitation into intellectual cogitation and rational argumentation. The Bible gives no philosophical treatment of human depravity. Is man totally or only partially depraved? Is he predestined to salvation or destruction or does he have the capacity within himself to accept or reject divine grace?[2] The Bible gives no clear and incontrovertible answer to these questions because they represent an intellectual cogitation on man as a 'substantive' and because they shift the focus of attention from flexible, moving narration of man-in-relation-to-God to abstract, propositional dogmatics. The dynamic movement of the Bible is formalized into a rational paradox, which the mind tries to resolve by taking one side or the other. The Bible begins with the assumption that man, man as sinner, man as

[1] Joseph Haroutunian, *Journal of Religion*, July, 1950, p. 232.

[2] The first, of course, is commonly represented by the difference between Augustinianism and Pelagianism; the second between Calvinism and Arminianism. For the first, cf. also the difference between II Bar. 54,15–19 and II Esd. 3.21–23; 4.30.

he is, is God's creature, created in his image, existing in constant dependence upon him. The meaning and destiny of his existence are determined entirely by this dependence and by what God is and does. Man's bondage and freedom cannot be held in tension but break up into contradictions except as they are seen as aspects of his relationship to the God who is his Lord in the immediacy of his existence.

From this theocentric viewpoint in which the fall, creation and redemption are held together, the Bible bears witness to the fact of sin as the chief characteristic of man's life in the world. It is not God's intention that this should be so. Man is no cosmic slave, as in Mesopotamia, in complete subjection to the reigning powers of the natural world, bound with all life into a rhythmic harmony, and carried along on the perennial tides of the cosmos. He possessed a servitude but it was one to be assumed and followed with the freedom of will which characterizes personality in God's image. He was not placed, as in Egypt, in a preordained station in a static universe which was not to be questioned.[1] He possessed a hitherto unknown freedom and a new burden of responsibility, honoured with the task of effectuating God's will. While a part of creation, he is separated from nature and made its king; and because he alone has the capacity to comprehend his creaturehood under God he understands himself to have been crowned with glory and honour, to have all things under his feet and alone to be the recipient of the divine visitation (Ps. 8). Yet this dignity and worth, conferred by God at creation, while the Bible's primary assumption about man, is nevertheless not the point of the Bible's concentration of attention. Instead, the chief concern is with the human tragedy, with the misery, guilt and alienation which is man's present lot.

[1] H. and H. A. Frankfort in *The Intellectual Adventure of Ancient Man*, Chicago, 1946, p. 370.

The Bible has no single comprehensive definition of sin. The latter is instead described in every sort of act, condition and intention.[1] It involves man's loss of power and stature as well as his punishment; it is committed against God and against man. One method of dealing with this variety in the Bible's testimony is to observe that it sees sin as both voluntarist and constituent. Sin is the result of man's will; it is his free act. But it is also imparted as an objective quantity. When it is one it is at the same time and immediately the other also. Where there is transgression, there is also material dislocation, a state of sinfulness. Adam transgresses; he knows he is naked; he is afraid; the earth is cursed. Sin as an act of the will has integral physical, psychical and social concomitants, including the corruption of the will itself.

Most catechisms define sin as disobedience against God and his 'law': that is, they stress the volitional element. This is likewise true of the Bible, though the central emphasis is typically not on transgression of a legal system in itself as the true root of sin but rather on the betrayal of the relationship with God.[2] In the story of the Fall sin is a willed act of dis-

[1] The attempt to comprehend the nature of sin by an etymological study of the words used for it is a common practice, but not a particularly helpful one. The fact is that the vocabulary for sin is almost identical, for the most part, with that used in Egypt, Babylon and Greece. Hence the nature of sin is to be understood from the vocabulary employed only when the terms are studied in the total context of the faith. Their content differs from that given them in paganism only because of the radical difference in the content of the faith.

[2] This is, of course, quite clear in the New Testament, where sin is represented as leaving the Father's house and living in the world apart from him (Luke 15.11ff.), as the betrayal of an infinite debt which man as a steward owes to his Master (Matt. 6.12; 18.23ff.), hence as the self-assertion of man in rebellion against God (e.g. Rom. 1.21–23). It is equally true of the Old Testament, even in those

obedience and thus the 'cause' of man's sin and sorrow. Yet in the story itself and throughout the centuries this 'first' sin has been used as a testimony to the constituent aspect of sin in human existence as we know it. It is the explanation of how, from the first and constantly, man lives in alienation from God and his fellow man, and at war with himself, while nature does not serve him as ideally as it should. The serpent as tempter hints at a constituent aspect of natural existence, outside of man, which tends to nullify the power of the will and cancel man's responsibility. Later on in the Bible the use of such terms as 'the sins of the fathers', 'the powers of darkness', 'Satan', and 'the flesh' all stress the conception of sin as a constituent aspect of man's life.

Yet, as in the story of the Fall, disobedience always remains the key word in the Bible. It is well summed up in the words of Jesus, weeping over Jerusalem, 'Ye would not' (Matt. 23.37). And because sin begins in disobedience, occasioned by a commandment, it is inescapably followed by judgment. It does not quietly lead to death, as might be the case if it were rooted in ignorance or finitude. The dependent, personal relationship is broken, and God responds actively in punishment, which is spiritual, social and material dislocation: i.e. sin in its constituent expression. To be sure, as St. Paul has it, death came through sin (Rom. 5.12); but this is death as the judgment of sin, to be overcome in God's role as Creator-Redeemer. In the Old Testament sin and sin's results are

passages where sin is either wholly sacramental in character or where the emphasis is upon the transgression of the Mosaic law. The reason is that behind such passages is the covenant conception, wherein all betrayal of the divine will is a breach of the personal relationship involved in the covenant. This is made especially clear in Deuteronomy, the seeming legalism of which is to be understood only in the light of the deep conception of the divine love which should call forth an unqualified obedient love on the part of the elect.

usually expressed by the same terms. The word 'evil', as a rendering of the Hebrew *ra'*, may mean volitional disobedience of God's moral will, the material effects of that disobedience, or both at the same time. Similarly, the ideas of sin and guilt, or of suffering and guilt, are not clearly distinguished because they are one with one another. Guilt is the accumulated result of a series of sins, a heavy burden which cannot be borne (Ps. 38.4) because the spiritual, physical or material judgment is its constituent aspect.[1]

One of the common biblical words which stresses the volitional aspect of sin is 'transgression' (Hebrew *pesha'*; Greek *adikeō*, *parabainō*, *anomeō* and *asebeō* among others). This term is preoccupied with intentions and acts, rather than with the results of activity. It conveys the conception of a divinely ordained order for human life. When man breaks this order, God punishes him. It is noteworthy that this rule of God is frequently recognized without being made explicit, that it was held to exist in tension with all human attempts to absolutize it in specific forms. Hence the term 'Law' is both the most general word for the divine teaching or direction and a specific name for the specific ordinances of the Mosaic covenant. This accounts for the double sense in which the term is used in the Pauline letters; and throughout the Bible only careful attention to the context can enable one to ascertain which aspect of the term is uppermost in a writer's mind. It is in the prophets and the New Testament that the term is least specific in designating the forms of the divine rule over human life. Yet it is in the prophets most of all that sin is characterized as 'transgression'. Sin, for them, is not human failure with respect solely to this legal item or that. It is

[1] Cf. Gottfried Quell, *Theologisches Wörterbuch zum Neuen Testament* (ed. by Gerhard Kittel), Band I, pp. 280–2 (in English, *Bible Key Words from Kittel*, III. *Sin*, London, 1951, pp. 21–3).

man's unwillingness to know his place and duty under God; it is rebellion.

Rebellion implies freedom, which the Bible assumes. It is, however, a freedom under God, for the normal expression of man's freedom is obedience and service. Freedom is God's gift to man to enable him to accept and fulfil his divinely given task. It is not a natural or absolute condition in itself. It is the ground of man's dignity, given *in order that* he may serve. In the designation of sin as 'transgression' the Bible testifies to man's abuse and rejection of his freedom because he has rejected the conception of creaturehood. The term attests man's choice of death in preference to life. Its rootage is the pride that assumes an anthropocentric security and that takes form in structures of power which enjoy the sanctions of idols. Precisely because of this type of sanction the idol-worshippers become enslaved, the victims of the work of their own hands. They cannot change what they have made and worshipped; only the living God can do a 'new thing'.

Inasmuch as human freedom in the Bible is God's gift, which is an expression of his 'image,' it follows that human freedom is real only in so far as God's freedom is complete. God gives that which he himself possesses. It is natural that, in stressing sin as rebellion and transgression, the prophets should underscore man's freedom, for it is they who give most eloquent testimony to the freedom of God. Theologically the significant meaning of what formerly has been called the prophetic 'discovery of monotheism' is that they bore witness to new dimensions of God's sovereignty and freedom. Israel's election was a free choice; it was not grounded in the people's 'genius for religion' or in moral excellence, but in grace. And the choice did not compromise God's freedom, for Israel's decision to be unfaithful meant her defeat rather than God's. The prophets did not so much preach purgation and

43

reform as death and resurrection. They anticipated the words of John the Baptist, 'God is able of these stones to raise up children unto Abraham' (Matt. 3.9).

Sin as transgression and rebellion is a willed act which impresses itself upon human life in all its aspects. Disobedience and its results are as inseparable as body and spirit in biblical psychology. The most common words for sin are the Hebrew *ḥeṭ'* (חֵטְא) with derivatives, together with the Greek synonym *hamartia* (ἁμαρτία). Sin in these terms is aberrant or wrong action, failure with respect to an objective norm. A sinner is one who has not met his stated obligations with respect to God and man. The magnitude of the failure and the results that follow are more important than the inner reasons for it. Sin in this sense makes man a debtor rather than a rebel. The sin must be paid for, either by the sinner or his 'redeemer'. Otherwise punishment will follow. Thus sinners must 'bear their sins', or others for them (e.g. the Servant 'bear the sin of many', Isa. 53.12). Similarly, in this emphasis the forgiveness of sin is presented as the cancellation of a debt or its vicarious payment by a redeemer ('I have blotted out . . . thy sins', Isa. 44.22; 'thou hast cast all my sins behind thy back,' Isa. 38.17). Just as sin in this sense of debt can be incurred both in one's relations with God and man, so both God and man may forgive it, except that man's failure in his relation with God cannot be atoned for by men. And here it is well to stress the fact that whenever the failures of man are dynamically related to their disobedience, purely human 'forgiveness' or restitution loses its significance. Ultimately all sin is against God and the only cure for it is 'the new birth'.[1]

[1] Not even Israel's sacrificial system was intended as an *opus operatum*, even though the prophets made clear that many so used it. A sacrifice by man effected atonement only because God had provided such a form as a means of grace and only when God deemed it

44

The conception of sin as aberrant action is often depreciated as being too external and impersonal. It materializes sin and reduces it to a matter of book-keeping; it is too closely related in its material aspects to archaic notions in primitive religion. Yet in its Biblical form this conception reminds us that the life of the spirit and the deeds of the will are material and constituent in their outcome. Sin manifests itself in material and social dislocations. Its results include warped personalities with darkened vision, and as well a darkened society. Sin, in short, becomes a constituent aspect of things as they are. Neither human life nor a human community can ever really begin anew on its own resources. The answer of the Bible to this exposure of 'individualism' is not despair, but a theocentric affirmation that 'God's arm is not shortened'. The power of the free Lord of creation is the measure of the power of his redemption.

The depth of Ps. 51 on sin, as of the Apostle Paul, consists in its capacity to hold the tragedy of material and natural perversion which is the result of sin together with the individual's immediate responsibility in transgression. Furthermore it affirms the intention and power of God to renew the penitent sinner in whose responsible existence and behaviour the whole burden of inherited sin enters experience and is expressed. Thus the Psalmist lives victoriously in the midst of his tragedy. Sin no longer has dominion over him (cf. Rom. 6.14); God can create a new heart. Yet in Ps. 51.5–8, as in Rom. 5.18, the objective and material character of sin as a

proper to accept it. In any case it was effective only for the unwitting sins of a faithful community. Sins committed with a high hand in a spirit of rebellion could receive no solace in sacrifice; in such case one could only throw himself in repentant spirit directly on the mercy of God. The forms of worship in themselves had no automatic efficacy; they were a means of grace only to the faithful.

corrosive factor in human nature is affirmed. Both share a common psychology, in which 'flesh' refers to human nature as a whole, while stressing its material expression. In becoming part of a scene in which by virtue of 'original sin' man lives at war with himself, with his fellows and with God, he nevertheless knows that involved in it is his own wilful transgression. The biblical testimony to sin as constituent warns against a spiritual perfectionism; but it likewise invests life's material realities with the redeeming power of God.

B. Society and the World

The constituent aspect of sin involves an assumption of man's social character, because by the mutual burden of transgression and failure the entire society of human life is warped. The world is estranged from God, existing under his judgment, filled with the turmoil of a sinning humanity; hence its end will come with a complete transformation (cf. Matt. 24; Mark 13; Luke 21; I Cor. 15.24).

1. Man as Social

Modern Christian individualism has tended to interpret the Gospel of the Kingdom in terms of an abstract universalism in which there is no place for the particularity of peoples. A nation of converted individuals, it is implied, will no longer exist in nationality but in universal brotherhood, for in Christ there is neither Jew nor Greek, bond or free. Hence the new humanity envisaged in the Gospel is believed to contain a great levelling process wherein all group distinctions are abolished; and this probably includes even the family, 'for in the resurrection they neither marry, nor are given in marriage' (Matt. 22.30). The truth in such a position is to be found in those New Testament passages which see the Kingdom as

46

healing those divisions among men which exist because society is alienated from God and thus is at enmity with itself. Yet it must be observed that social organisms are not condemned because they are social but because so many of them accentuate the alienation. It is the latter which is the focus of attention, not the former.

The fact is that the Bible presents no conception of individual man as existing in and for himself, nor does it know an abstract universalism in which the individual's relation to God rather than the problem of society is the focus of attention. On the contrary, the individual was created for society— 'One man is no man' ('Ein Mensch ist kein Mensch'),[1] for he is man only in the midst and as a member of a group. There is no man apart from a people in which he lives and moves and has his being. The problem of sin is its disruptive character within society, or else its ability to subject a whole society to demonic forces and demonic ends.

Man's social nature is something assumed in the New Testament, and can only be demonstrated by the description of the new community formed by and in Jesus Christ (see Chap. III). This community inherited primary assumptions about common life from Hebrew culture. The fellowship of the twelve disciples was modelled upon that of the rabbi and his disciples or 'learners' in Judaism.[2] They had accepted the solemn call to discipleship and the renunciation of all other ties; they had entered into a special relationship,

[1] L. Köhler, *Theologie des Alten Testaments*, 2nd Impression, Tübingen, 1947, p. 113.

[2] The only explicit reference to this type of fellowship in Old Testament prophecy is Isa. 8.16. The fellowship of the 'sons of the prophets' around Samuel and Elisha, the Rechabites, and the later Jewish Covenanters (as known from the Dead Sea Scrolls and 'Zadokite' document) are further examples.

were bound up in a unity with their Master, had received from him a derivative authority to preach and cast out demons, and by virtue of the master-disciple unity were expected to share the fate of their master. Organically related to this fellowship was the larger community of the brotherhood, sharing the life of its Lord ('there am I in the midst of them', Matt. 18.20), his sufferings, power and authority, participating in the covenant-meal, and united in a bond stronger than natural ties. In this perspective, disloyalty to the Lord is a terrible crime, the chief of sins, as evidenced by the remorse of Peter and the suicide of Judas (Mark 14.72; Matt. 27.3–10).[1] It involves not only the conception of disloyalty but also the disruption of the community, for denial of the Lord and disobedience to his commands are one and the same thing and result in the defiling of the community (cf., e.g. Matt. 6.24; 7.21–23; 10.33; Acts 5.1–11; I Cor. 5–6).

In the Old Testament the conception of the community in covenant with its Lord involved the same type of mutuality and sharing of life. Community is a psychic harmony of individual souls, held together by mutual vows in covenant with its Lord and sharing the common blessing which he confers. The harmony of will is not a simple agreement of a horizontal type, but a conforming of all wills to that of the Lord in a mutuality of commitment which results in a oneness of heart and life, in a psychic unity. Hence idolatry is the chief of sins, not merely because it is a formal disloyalty but because the covenant unity is broken in the denial of him whose will and blessing creates and sustains the community.[2]

[1] See further Holt Graham, 'Community in the Synoptic Gospels' in *The Joy of Study* (ed. by Sherman E. Johnson), New York, 1951, pp. 31–42.

[2] Contrary to common opinion, capital punishment is rarely a penalty in Israelite law. That it is commanded for enticement into

Such a conception was a theological development from early folk society. Biblical faith always preserved to a large extent its ties with a patriarchal type of nomadic life, largely in reaction against current agrarianism and urbanism. Hence the ideal society was conceived in a nostalgic vein to be the simple and uncomplicated order of patriarchal times. In such an order the basic unit was the family, which merged into the clan without clear lines of demarcation, as the clan merged into the tribe and tribe into people. Thus the conception of 'the children of Israel' as a term for the people involved a psychic unity and was traditionally simplified after the patriarchal pattern by the assumption of a common ancestor. In New Testament times the unity of the brotherhood and the unity of ancestry became a point of controversy, but even in the Gentile Church continuity with the old ideal was preserved in the teaching that Christians are children of Abraham by faith and adoption, and heirs of the promises.

Reflection on the meaning of creation, furthermore, led to the assertion that man is social by his very creation. The Hebrew word, *'adam* (אָדָם), used in the creation stories, is a peculiarly biblical word which appears to designate man in both his individual and collective aspects, and can be used for both. In Gen 1. *'adam* is the general term, but male and female are its components. In Gen. 2 an older document uses the term

idolatry (Deut. 13.1–18; 17.2–7) appears to us as terribly severe. Yet when the nature of Israelite community is understood, we can at least comprehend the reason for the severity. Other prescriptions of the death penalty were for premeditated murder (Deut. 19.11–13), for the worthless son who disrupted the unity of the family (Deut. 21.18–21), for certain sexual abuses (22.13–25) and for making merchandise of a fellow Israelite (24.7). In Deuteronomy the usual phrase explaining the punishment is: 'So shalt thou purge evil from the midst of thee.'

in a slightly different manner; the *'adam* is not sufficient in himself, woman is his counterpart, and the two together become 'one flesh' (i.e. one person). Jesus in quoting Gen. 1.27 and 2.24 adds the words: 'so that they are no more two, but one flesh' (Mark 10.6–8). Marriage involves that union of souls without which neither of the sexes is complete and in which the love of the other is the same as the love of self (so Eph. 5.28–31; cf. I Cor. 6.16). The social nature of the human individual is thus vividly clear, because by creation he is meant to adjust himself to the 'thou' of the opposite sex. He is incomplete in his individuality; 'it is not good that the man should be alone' (Gen. 2.18).

The essential social nature of man is further shown in the dread, fear and consequent 'curse' of loneliness. Lack of community is unnatural, a constituent aspect of sin, and an actual curse. It was a part of the curse put upon Cain: not only was he not to be able to raise crops from the ground, but he was to be a fugitive and wanderer, the lonely exile, a man without a people (Gen. 4). The 'individualism' of Jeremiah, Ezekiel, Job, and the authors of the psalms of lament is a terrible burden laid upon them; it is the loneliness of suffering ('I sat alone because of thy hand,' Jer. 15.17), and the cause of the bitterness of their laments.

So strong is this dread and curse of an anti-social existence that despite strong tendencies to repudiate the unregenerate or natural society there are no typical cases of individual asceticism in the Bible (see Chap. IV). The Rechabites of the Old Testament, the Essenes and the pre-Christian Jewish Covenanters possessed monastic characteristics, but they were communal societies, intensely conscious of the psychic unity of their brotherhoods. Elijah and John the Baptist were men whose lonely state was no end in itself, but something imposed by God as a part of a special calling to a disrupted society which had denied its Lord. The very intensity of the calls of Jeremiah and Jesus, both of whom were misunderstood and opposed by their own townsmen, can be measured against this background of family-clan solidarity and the consequent curse of having to stand alone against it.[1]

Thus man and society are not opposing concepts but are involved in one another. Behind every individual is a community because it is man's nature to communicate himself to others and to share blessing with them. Community is a unity of soul and will, but the individual is not lost in it; 'it does not consist in obliterating the individual, but in imbuing him with the common character and spirit of the community'.[2] Rather than being lost in the social group, he is instead found in it, attaining his true selfhood by sharing its purposes and partaking of its well-being (*shalom*). To belong to community is to share the life of a 'people', and the conception of 'people' arose from the understanding of kinship, starting in the father's household, extending to the family, and finally to all kinsmen who take part in the whole of the common history.

When such a conception of man in society is maintained, then the social nature of sin is more easily understood. Every sin ultimately involves the society of the sinner, and a sinful act is one through which society is dissolved. Either an internal attitude of hatred and falsehood or an external act which results from them is a breach of the psychic unity of community. Guilt, vanity or emptiness, and social dissolution are all involved in sin's constituent aspect. Falsehood, violence and vanity are part of one another and an important aspect of sin, because they proceed from the formless emptiness of a

[1] See further Johs. Pedersen, *Israel* I–II, Copenhagen and London, 1926, pp. 263ff.

[2] *Ibid.*, p. 57.

51

chaotic soul which 'cannot work anything, but only dissolve',[1] which cannot love and thus link itself to the community, but only make the heart hard or the neck stiff and thus disrupt community.

The biblical understanding of the 'peoples' and the 'world' proceeds from this conception of man in society. Since God is the Lord of all men, the source of all blessing and 'peace' (shalom, social wholeness, well-being), society can only exist as it derives its inner unity from him and as it acknowledges its complete dependence, its complete obedience, and its unwavering loyalty to its Head. Kinship, the father's household, and covenant kingdom were employed for the understanding of the whole relation of heaven and earth, but the sin of man has dissolved the communion of wills in this divine organization of beings. Yet the vitality and strength of a people or social order which does not acknowledge the sovereignty of God must still be explained. The Bible does this by assuming either that the organism is given this power temporarily to accomplish a negative or positive work for God in history,[2] or else it is under the temporary dominion of spiritual beings who possess a demonic character. To this aspect of the biblical conception of the world we must now turn.

2. Nationality and the World

The peoples or nations of the earth (hag-goyim, ta ethne) receive in the Bible both positive and negative evaluation.

---

[1] Ibid., p. 413.

[2] E.g. God's 'hardening' of Pharaoh's heart at the time of the Exodus that his own name be exalted in the earth; the Deuteronomic belief that some of the peoples in Canaan at the time of the conquest were not destroyed in order that they might 'prove' Israel (Judg. 2.21–23); the prophetic conception of Assyria, Babylon and Persia as divine agents; the Pauline belief in the positive nature of Roman government and law (Rom. 13); etc.

In as much as they exist, it is felt that they must have behind them an affirmation of God. In as much as they are alienated from God and serve their hand-made idols, they are under the divine condemnation. These two aspects of the biblical viewpoint are both involved in the reference attributed to the Apostle Paul in Acts 14.15-17: namely, that the Creator 'in times past suffered all nations to walk in their own ways' though never leaving himself without witness in his steady blessing of the cycle of nature. The words are both an attack upon the idolatry of the nations and an affirmation of the purpose of God in permitting their existence (cf. Rom. 1). As to whether nationality will continue to exist in the Kingdom of God is a question to which the Bible gives no clear answer. In Rev. 7.9 we read of the host of martyrs 'of all nations, and kindreds, and people, and tongues,' who stand before the throne of the God, clothed in white robes. In the New Jerusalem the glory of God will enlighten the world, and 'the nations of them which are saved shall walk in the light of it; and the kings of the earth do bring their glory and honour into it' (21.24). In it are the river of life and the tree of life 'for the healing of the nations' (22.2).

The author of the Apocalypse does not give the impression of speaking directly to the question of nationality versus universalism; he simply assumes that nations and kings will continue to exist when the New Jerusalem is the centre of the world. The life which proceeds from the city, however, will heal the alienation of the nations so that the whole world will be united in it.

This form of thought is taken directly from the eschatological sections of Old Testament prophecy. There too it is affirmed that all peoples will flow to the New Jerusalem, and, having acknowledged the sovereignty of God, will be instructed in his ways with the result that universal harmony among the nations will be brought into being (Isa. 2.2–4; Micah 4.1–4; cf. Isa. 60; 66.18, 23.) Even Egypt and Assyria, after the Day of Judgment has fallen on them, will be turned to God, who will then bless them, 'saying, "Blessed be Egypt my people, and Assyria the work of my hands, and Israel mine inheritance" ' (Isa. 19.25). In Ezekiel the acts of God both in judgment and salvation are all to the end that his name be acknowledged and glorified, not only in Israel, but among all peoples (e.g. 36.36; 37.28). In the prophecies against foreign nations in the Book of Jeremiah, the Day of the Lord is believed to be about to fall on all the nations of the civilized world, but it is noteworthy that after the terrible judgment at least certain of them will be restored, as will be the case with Israel (Jer. 48.47; 49.6, 39).

In other words, while the matter is not clearly reasoned, biblical eschatology does not appear to contemplate the abolition of nationality.[1] The conception of man's social

[1] It is possible, of course, that this is a misunderstanding of the biblical, or at least of the New Testament's, language. One member of the Chicago committee feels that both views (the abolition of nationality and its retention) can be found in a literal interpretation of eschatological passages. Yet when the factor of language is considered, it can be argued that the references to nations and races in the new age are simply accommodating modes of expression, derived from Old Testament prophecy where there were no other terms available, and hence suggesting nothing regarding the composition of the Kingdom. Professor Aimo T. Nikolainen of Helsinki, after reading this section, has written: 'I have taken for granted that the parousia of Christ or the Last Judgment would put an end to the national divisions . . . , that at the Last Judgment men are gathered as nations for the last time (Matt. 25.31–33). In the eternal life there is only one nation, one family. . . . However, it is possible that the teaching of the Bible is not quite uniform at this point. On the other hand, the Revelation (7.9; 21.24; 22.2) can also be interpreted to mean that while all nations will be represented in the New Jerusalem, there is actually only one nation, the New Israel.'

nature is too deeply fixed; and this includes not only the individual's position within a family but also the sense of his belonging to a people. In fact, the divine affirmation to the existence of separate peoples seems clearly to be the sense of Gen. 9-10. In the latter Israel's place among a great family of peoples is presented. All are kinsmen through the ancestor Noah, and descended from his three sons. All are recipients of the blessing contained in the covenant with Noah (8.20-22; 9.1-19); and all are involved in the special blessing given Israel (12.3; cf. Jer. 4.2). Yet the story of the Tower of Babel in Gen. 11 gives another perspective to the problem of nations and races. There the splitting of mankind into groups with different languages is viewed as a divine curse because of the pride of men who refuse to acknowledge their creature-hood. In this case nationality is seen to proceed, not from any idea of the family or kingdom of God, but from a basic spiritual structure in which human power is perverted from its created purpose. Sin has resulted in a separation of men, not only from God, but from each other.

It is characteristic of the realism of Old Testament faith that this vexing double aspect of nationality, which defies any simple harmonization, seems to characterize the whole movement of its history.[1] The same priestly writer who in Genesis so emphasizes the special place of God's eternal covenant with Israel (Gen. 17), also insists upon the direct dependence of all peoples upon God. In the blessing and covenant of Noah all mankind is the bearer, not only of God's peaceful will, but also of his command against the shedding of human blood, 'for in the image of God made he man' (Gen. 9.6). Hence all men are held responsible for this ordinance, including both Israel and the nations. In this light Israel can be condemned for being even more wilful than the nations in disobedience to the

[1] See Walther Eichrodt, *Gottes Volk und die Völker*, Basel, 1942, p. 7.

divine ordinances (Ezek. 5), for all are held together in a divinely directed history. Thus Noah in the name of the God of Shem can express both blessing and curse upon Shem, Japhet and Canaan; and Amos can proclaim God's leading of the Philistines and Aramaeans from their respective homelands as in a sense comparable to his leading of Israel from Egypt (Amos 9.7).

The problem of the nations is clearly illustrated in the oracles against Tyre and Egypt in the Book of Ezekiel (chaps. 27–32). Chapter 27 describes the capital of the great Phoenician trading empire in all the unsurpassed glory which God intended it to have. The rich trade of the whole world belonged to it, and 'thou wast filled, and made very glorious in the midst of the seas' (27.25). Indeed, 'Thou has been in Eden the garden of God . . . perfect in thy ways from the day that thou wast created, till iniquity was found in thee' (28.13–15). But the trouble is that the power and wealth of this great city have led its king to say: 'I am a God; I sit in the seat of God. . . . Yet thou art a man, and not God, though thou set thine heart as the heart of God' (28.2). Similarly Pharaoh of Egypt was a mighty cedar, in beauty and height surpassing even the trees of Eden. In his branches the birds nested; 'under his shadow dwelt all great nations'. Yet the trouble is that 'his heart is lifted up in his height', and he shall 'be brought down with the trees of Eden unto the nether parts of the earth' (chap. 31).

The self-deification of the powerful is the reason for the divine condemnation of the nations. They will not acknowledge dependency. Why is this so? A few writers in the Old Testament go further than the mere assertion of pride, and penetrate deep within the metaphysical background of history in order to discover the reason for the particularity and power of nationality. Psalm 82 affirms God's sovereignty over all peoples and his right to demand of them adherence to his law. Their gods are his agents, delegated to rule, but here, it is affirmed, God has called them to an accounting for their failure to provide justice with the result that 'the foundations of the earth are shaken'. Hence they are condemned to death like a mortal. Deuteronomy 32.8, in the midst of a proclamation of God's providential acts in Israel's behalf during 'the days of old', reads:

> When the Most High gave the nations their inheritance,
>   When he separated the children of men,
> He fixed the realms of the peoples
>   According to the number of the sons of God (LXX).

Here the peoples are understood to be in subjection to heavenly powers. 'The separation of the children of men into peoples and the determination of their boundaries goes hand in hand with their religious particularity, indeed obtains in the latter their peculiar appointed power'.[1] The Book of Daniel understands the nations to be under the guidance of angelic powers who engage in conflicts for their respective nations and thus play a fateful role in the division of mankind (10.13, 20–21; 11.1; 12.1). Hence in the world judgment which is to come Isa. 24.21 affirms the punishment of God, not only upon the kings of the earth, but upon 'the host of the height on high' (cf. Jer. 46.25).

Nationality in the Old Testament is thus comprehended in two ways. On the one hand, it is a proper expression of man's social existence and is the recipient of the divine blessing. On the other hand, the nature of its divisions, each of which possesses a peculiar power, cannot be understood solely by

[1] *Ibid.*, p. 8. Cf. also Deut. 4.19. The original text of Deut. 33.3a probably contained a similar idea.

geographical and sociological factors, but by the deeper religious springs of its power which both bind it into one and give it individuality of expression. The enmity between nations and their enmity with God finds its ultimate rootage at this deeper spiritual level. For this reason, the later translators who rendered the Hebrew *goyim* as 'the heathen' were not without their justification, for the ultimate riddle of the nations is that alienation against God which is comprehended in the Bible under the category of the demonic.

By New Testament times this conception of the spiritual power existing in and explaining the character of the world powers had become more coherent and explicit. Two factors of especial importance may be mentioned. One was the conception of 'world' (or 'universe') as expressed in the term 'cosmos' taken over from Greek antiquity. This term is an abstraction which enabled men to think of the whole unredeemed world without emphasis upon the particularity of peoples. The Old Testament possessed no comparable term, but speaks more concretely of kings, peoples and nations, who indeed were more numerous as independent entities than in the world dominated by Rome. To be sure, the term 'cosmos' ('world') did not possess the same connotations in the Greek philosophies and in Judaism or the New Testament. In the latter, it is used for the creation of God the Creator, and most frequently, not so much in a cosmological sense, as in the meaning 'the world of men', denoting 'the quintessence of earthly conditions of life and earthly possibilities. It embraces all the vicissitudes included between the pairs of polar terms "life . . . death", "things present . . . things future" (I Cor. 3.22).'[1]

A second factor is the developed view of Satan and the

[1] Rudolf Bultmann, *Theology of the New Testament*, Vol. I, (tr. by Kendrick Grobel), New York, London 1951, p. 254.

fallen angels which arose in intertestamental times. While they do not constitute a dominant emphasis of New Testament writing, which is uninterested in cosmological speculation, they nevertheless are in the background as something assumed which explained the power and character of historical evil, both individual and social. Furthermore, the world's enmity and alienation now has focus in a single dominion; that of Satan.

With the presence of these two factors, largely missing from the Old Testament, the early Church was enabled to conceive of the 'cosmos' or 'world' (in the sense defined above) in a manner which indicated a definite theological judgment. The world at present is under Satan's power, in subjection to the principalities and powers of darkness (Rom. 8.38; I Cor. 15.24–5; Eph. 2.2–3; 3.10). Thus Satan can presume that it is in his power to give Christ 'all the kingdoms of this world and the glory of them' if he so chooses (Matt. 4.8–9). The New Testament abounds with descriptions of the terrible individual and social discord which exists in the world thus dominated, of which Rom. 1.18–32 is perhaps the most detailed and vivid. There, as in the Old Testament, the thought begins not with primitive savages but with the men of a highly civilized world, whose arrogance leads them to idolatry, to the senseless worship of objects *within* creation (vv. 20–25). The relationship of man and 'God having thus been violated, both the individual and society have been filled with the most horrible disharmony. Passionate perversions come into being; the relationship between the sexes becomes unnatural (vv. 26–27); and society is turned into a wilderness of strife (vv. 28–31). Yet as in the Old Testament it is assumed that all men are responsible for this situation. They know the decree of God that all 'which commit such things are worthy of death'; nevertheless they not only do them but have pleasure in those who do them (v. 32; cf. Rom. 2.14–15; Gen. 9.5–6).

In the New Testament, therefore, moral fatalism is not the result of Satan's dominion. Man may be in slavery to him and to his forces, who include 'the elemental spirits of the cosmos', but it is a slavery by man's own choice and it is a condition which will not last forever. Over against 'this world' there now stands Christ's Kingdom, and man is confronted with the possibility of choosing his Lord in the knowledge that 'this world' has been judged and will come to its end (John 12.31; I Cor. 7.31). The Apostle Paul seems to imply that even subjection to the Jewish Law is in some measure equivalent to the slavery under 'the elemental spirits', but God has sent forth his Son to redeem those under the law and to save them from a bondage to beings who by nature are no-gods and who by Christ are shown to be 'weak and beggarly elemental spirits' (Gal. 4.1–11).[1]

The New Testament view of the world thus contains a fundamental ambiguity which can only be adjusted when the world is viewed from its varied aspects under God. On the one hand, it is God's creation and he has never abdicated his sovereignty. On the other hand, it is the domain of demonic powers. Yet these powers also owe their being to God, and their present alienation from him is the objectification of the world's alienation, in both its individual and structural aspects. This point of view seems to have prevented the early Church from surrendering completely to an apocalypticism which gave up all sense of any value existing in the world of this æon. To be sure, the Johannine literature and Revelation give an impression of having surrendered this value, though in different ways, but the Church as a whole never succumbed

[1] Cf. Bo Reicke, 'The Law and this World According to Paul' in *Journal of Biblical Literature*, Vol. LXX, 1951, pp. 259–76.

entirely either to a 'realized' eschatology or to an immediate end of the whole creation in apocalyptic terms (see further Chap. IV). It is important that we should distinguish between hope and value in this age. The New Testament has no hope which is based upon the permanence of this age. The fallen cosmos will end that its alienation may be removed. Yet God is Lord of this cosmos as it is. There is, for example, a positive value in the Law, even in the mind of Paul, because God who gave it, whether directly or through the mediation of angels (Gal. 3.19-20), intended it for good. It is 'holy and just and good', and a tutor unto Christ, even though the Christian must understand that in itself it cannot give life but instead furnishes the occasion for sin to work death (Rom. 7.7-25; Gal. 3.21-26). Furthermore, though the Gentiles do not know the Law in its Mosaic form, they 'do by nature what the law requires' and show that this requirement is 'written on their hearts' (Rom. 2.14-15). Thus Roman government and Roman law cannot be said to be a total evil. Such authority could not exist except it had been instituted by God, and it should be respected and obeyed (Rom. 13)—at least in its positive aspect.[1]

[1] In a different occasion when the demonic aspect of Roman power was most virulent, Christians were to view the matter differently, as in the Book of Revelation. That angelic or demonic powers were believed to stand behind the state seems clear in the Pauline letters, and it has been argued that while I Cor. 2.7-8 and 6.3 conceive of them in their negative aspect, Rom. 13 emphasizes their positive function under God's dominion: see Bo Reicke, *op. cit.*, pp. 269-70 and literature there cited, especially Oscar Cullmann, *Christ and Time* (tr. by F. V. Filson), Philadelphia, London, 1952, pp. 194ff. Whether this is the correct interpretation of Rom. 13 is debated, but ultimately the meaning must be the same whether the authorities are the human officials or the spiritual powers behind them: God through them works in a positive manner as well as negatively.

It is thus clear that the New Testament's view of the 'world' is no more subject to a simple harmonization than is that of the Old Testament. Throughout the Scripture, history is seen to move by God's direction, through his 'Yea' and 'Nay'. Man's sin is both voluntarist and constituent, and both individual and social. For these reasons man cannot rely on his own innate capacity, nor upon his social structures, in order to find fulness of life, for both he and they are under the divine condemnation. Yet the world, alienated as it is and in slavery to spiritual powers, is still God's world, and man is still God's creature and the recipient of his grace in Christ. For this reason, the Bible permits no moral quietism, for, as God is the active Sovereign even of sinful man and sinful society, his blessing is to be seen in our midst, even amongst those who refuse to acknowledge him.

III

THE REDEMPTIVE ACTS OF GOD:
THE NEW MAN AND
THE NEW SOCIETY

IF we were in a position to ask an Isaiah, an Ezra, or a Peter about the 'new society' and about the relation of individual and community within it, it is doubtful whether we should receive answers completely satisfying to us. The problem of the alienation between man and society in modern times is *our* problem, and we cannot simply assume that it was likewise a problem to biblical man. Our task in the first instance is simply to put ourselves in his position, in so far as we can, in order to understand why the contradiction between man and society did not exist in the sense that it does for us.

In the various social and political philosophies of our day there is a large area of agreement regarding both the problem of man's life and its solution. Regardless of the great differences in viewpoint the problem is generally seen to lie in the area of man's alienation from society, and the solution proposed is usually to the effect that *man* must create the *new* society. The failure of both democratic liberalism and Marxism thus far to create their ideal communities has left its mark in the strong undercurrent of pessimism and of cynical disregard for the classical virtues. Among intellectuals, at least, Utopia is no longer the great dream, for the mental climate which could produce it and believe in it has radically changed.

A. The New Society as God's Creation

In the Bible the answer to the human problem is the new man and the new society which God creates. An unqualified optimism or pessimism regarding human possibilities is avoided, but hope remains constant because faith has been generated. This faith is not grounded primarily in any doctrinaire position as to what man can or cannot do, but is instead based upon the unlimited possibilities of God. That the power of God is unlimited, his creative work demonstrates so fully. Of all the biblical symbols of this power, perhaps the most vivid is that depicting his control of Leviathan (Job 41; cf. 26.12–13; Ps. 74.12ff.; Isa. 27.1). The latter was the mythological monster of the deep in Canaanite religion and one of the figures behind the Beast in the Book of Revelation. He was the great symbol of primordial chaos whose destruction or control was the pre-requisite of world order. Yet before God his power is nothing; God alone can command and the serpent obeys (cf. Amos 9.3). God alone is almighty, he alone can do what he wills. His cosmic work was to biblical man an objective fact, one to be acknowledged anterior to the certainties of intuition or mysticism. God existed before human experience and neither he nor his work is confined to it. Hence man is constrained to reverence, to a fear or awe of the Lord, to humility before that gigantic concentration of power which he can do nothing whatever to control.

Biblical man had arrived at the unitary view of ultimate power, not through speculative thought, but through his knowledge of the meaning of history. A new community had been brought into being amidst the opposition of earthly powers. A people had been formed from that which had been 'no-people'. Within a weak and oppressed group there suddenly appeared power. To the civilized world the God of

64

Israel could have been nothing more than the minor deity of a minor people. But to Israel he was the Lord who had delivered her from the house of bondage, had given her a land of milk and honey, and in doing so had shown his power over nature, Pharaoh and the armies of Canaan. The Unknown God was Lord indeed, and his visitation of Israel as 'the God of the fathers' illumined the true meaning of the ancestral traditions. For some reason, clearly known only to himself, God had selected one people out of all the families of the earth as recipients of his special guidance, until in the events of the Exodus, Sinai and the conquest of Canaan he had brought them into being as a new nation which owed its existence solely to him. Life now became unthinkable apart from him. He was Lord of the community, the source of its unity, the promise of its life, the God whose 'righteous' acts in Israel's behalf men shall rehearse (Judg. 5.11, cf. I Sam. 12.7ff.). 'Happy art thou, O Israel; who is like unto thee— a people saved by the Lord' (Deut. 33.29).

The formative events of the people's history thus showed that God alone was Lord of all things and further that the unlimited power of God was employed by him in a redemptive manner. His unmerited love was as remarkable as his strength. The fear and reverence which his power induced were coupled with joy, thanksgiving and deep affection because his acts showed his nature to be redemptive. Central to biblical man's consciousness was an awareness that a new society had actually been brought into being on this earth and it was an act of God as significant as creation itself. Furthermore, the manner in which the society was formed was so extraordinary that its individual members were drawn into an intimate, personal and affectional relationship with the Lord who loved them. This relationship was given formal expression in covenant rites, but central to it was a personal attachment in which joy, love and reverence were combined as the mainspring from which duty proceeded. Sin now became a violation of personal attachment, so that to the sense of aberration and guilt were added the deeper and emotional feelings of infidelity, betrayal of love and trust. Repentance and forgiveness of sin could thus touch the individual's innermost being with the result that true atonement could never be pure expiation apart from reconciliation, renewed blessing and promise of life.

That Israel did not attain the fulness of new life because the individual was not redeemed from sin did not mean that she ceased to hope. Her failure led the prophets to proclaim not only God's wrath but also his promised forgiveness and reconstitution. She had been redeemed from Pharaoh's bondage in times past, and the future would see her redeemed again, this time both from enemies and from sin itself. God's punishment would be a purifying fire, his forgiveness would be accompanied by the gift of a new heart and a new spirit (e.g. Ezek. 36). Hope lay in faith, not in human capacity; man's failure served to purify him of idolatry. Tragedy had redemption within it.

These views were the heritage of the Christian Church. The latter like Israel before it was aware of itself as a new community which God, not man, had created. Conscious both of its weakness and of its power, it explained the one by sin and the other by God. The most extraordinary thing in history is not simply the evil and the alienation of the world but rather the work of God the Redeemer to reconcile the world to himself. This work has taken place in a certain specified time and among one people; it began with Abraham but it has been fulfilled, it has culminated in Christ. And the Church is the fellowship of those who have been gathered together as in a flock by the Lord, who acknowledge the special work of God for what it is, who have been led to surrender to the Lordship of the risen Christ, who following him take upon themselves the burden of his world's sin, live in him by the power of the spirit, and proclaim to the world God's mighty acts over sin, Satan and the principalities of darkness.

To the pagan world Israel undoubtedly appeared as simply one small nation among many others, while the early Church was probably considered as just another of the Jewish sects or another of the many mystery cults which held out the promise of salvation to their initiates. Among the pagan cults there were dying-rising gods, from whose flesh power was transferred to the believer in cultic ceremonies. Yet the features which sharply distinguish the biblical community have since been fully recognized. Central among them is not simply the biblical penetration into 'the deeper realities of the spirit', but instead, in the first instance at least, the function of history and of living historical memory in the creation, preservation and renewal of life and community.

This means that as distinct from pagan societies, and even from the modern Church, biblical community had a very real sense of the meaning and manner of its formation in historical events. These events were not ordinary; they were accompanied by the signs and wonders of God.[1] In both the

[1] Some biblical theologians are insisting strongly today that the acts of God are visible only to faith. These theologians appear to object to the location of revelation in history because to do so would base the revelation on 'objective' evidence rather than on faith alone; it would lead one to trust a 'process' rather than God. The current attack on *Heilsgeschichte* (the conception of the Bible as centred in the saving acts of God in a particular history) seems in part to be motivated by this viewpoint. Yet such an exclusive and one-sided emphasis may fail to do justice to the biblical understanding of the 'objective' nature of God's acts. These are historical events interpreted and understood by faith, to be sure, but they are none the less real events

67

Old and New Testaments the central affirmation is concerned with God's *saving work* to the end that he might create a people for himself (e.g. I Pet. 2.9–10). The community thus formed was united in common worship in which the central act was a confessional recital of what had happened, accompanied by expressions of joy, praise and thanksgiving, by interpretative statements or exposition of the meaning of what had been confessed, and by reaffirmation of loyalty to the Lord who was the community's Ruler. In other words, biblical people really believed that they had been saved by God through his historical work. God's salvation had made them into a people and had bound them to himself. And this belief was kept alive as the chief constituting factor of community life because it was kept central in worship.

As illustrations of this fact, we note first the Lord's Supper on the one hand, and the chief festivals of Israel, on the other. The elements of the Supper communicate God's redemptive work in Christ ('my body which is broken for you') and as well the new fellowship which Christ's offering of himself has created ('this cup is the new covenant in my blood'). Furthermore, the celebration of the meal is to serve as a memorial of Christ's act and a testimony to his future work.[1]

which cannot be etherealized or relegated to the realm of the 'spiritual'. Biblical realism consists precisely in its refusal to separate a spiritual realm, known only to faith, from the real world known only to the senses. There is only one creation and one God who makes himself known in it, not by the gift of a spiritual *gnosis*, but by the evidence of his *activity*.

[1] Objection has been raised by a European scholar to this statement because it appears to emphasize the past and future tenses to the exclusion of the present. He says: 'Is not the real presence of Christ, His actuality in the Eucharist, equally important? As God was present at the great feasts of Israel, so Christ is present in the midst of His people who come in His name in order to receive his body and blood.' In

'This do in remembrance of me. . . . For as oft as ye eat this bread, and drink this cup, ye do show the Lord's death till he come' (I Cor. 11.23–26). In other words, the worshipping community by means of this sacrament recalls God's redemptive work in Christ as forming a new fellowship, and in so doing finds its covenant bond renewed and its hope established. Historical memory in sacramental participation purifies and strengthens the new society ('whoseoever shall eat this bread and drink the cup of the Lord unworthily shall be guilty of the body and blood of the Lord', I Cor. 11.27). The bond which draws the members together into an organism is thus of the strongest possible kind, provided that the reality of

answer to this objection it may be said that the emphasis here is upon the efficacy of the memorial feast to form and sustain community in the present as well as in the past. Hence in the context of this discussion it is affirmed that the present realization of and identification with the saving drama binds the members into a unity through memory, present participation and hope. There is no need for the biblical writers to make a special point of the 'real presence' of God or of Christ in festival or sacrament; and *they do not do so.* God is the living God; Christ is the living Christ; and both are present in the work of the Spirit. Protestantism has found it necessary to lay special emphasis on the 'real presence' because of its controversy with Roman Catholic magical ideas. But has this controversy always been wise? Has it not encountered the danger of placing emphasis upon the wrong point, a point which the biblical writers took for granted because they had a real doctrine of the Spirit, while they stressed the elements of memorial and communion in the New Covenant? We must always be aware of the subtle danger of converting the sacraments into typical pagan festivals by our failure to emphasize sufficiently the distinctively biblical emphases. It is true that the Lord's Supper and Passover were more than simple memorial services because they were acts of worship and renewals of covenant within the called community. Hence the Protestant doctrine of the 'real presence' if it is biblically centred, must be defined precisely by what is written on these pages, and not as something to be added to what is here presented.

God's act in Christ is actually the living, dominant element in the faith. Past, present and future are all held together in a worship that sustains community because it affirms what God did in Christ, what he is now doing and will do, and because the emphasis is not upon the outward, semi-magical ritual so characteristic of pagan cults but instead upon forgiveness, inner purification and a personal attachment of the most intimate kind.

In Israel every male was required to appear 'before the Lord' at the central sanctuary three times each year (Exod. 23.17; 34.23; Deut. 16.16). These were at Passover and the feast of unleavened bread in the spring, at the feast of weeks or first-fruits fifty days later, and at the feast of ingathering or booths in the fall. All three of these festivals had an agricultural background, but as celebrated in Israel their meaning was transformed. Passover and unleavened bread were early joined as a festival commemorating the deliverance from Egypt when Israel as the covenant nation was brought into being (cf. Exod. 12–13). The feast of weeks or first-fruits acknowledged God as Owner of the land to whom a portion of its produce belonged. An early confession, which the worshipper made when he presented a basket of first-fruits, is preserved in Deut. 26.5–10. It recites the redemptive history in which God 'saw our affliction', 'brought us forth out of Egypt with a mighty hand', 'brought us into this place, and hath given us this land, a land flowing with milk and honey'. The autumn festival of ingathering of summer fruits became, by Deuteronomic times at least, the feast of booths, commemorating again the escape from Egypt (Deut. 16.13, cf. Lev. 23.41–43).

The Hebrew word for feast or festival in these instances (*hag*) actually means 'pilgrimage' for common worship as a nation at the central sanctuary. The three main national 'feasts' were thus times of joy and thanksgiving to God for having brought the nation into being by saving acts and for giving it a land in which to live. They were also occasions when vows of loyalty were taken, and offerings of praise, confession and communion made.[1] Yet it is to be noted that, whatever the type of worship, the sense of history was dominant. The worshipper was continually exhorted to affirm: 'We are a people saved and made into a nation; we must hearken and obey the Lord who has been thus gracious unto us.' And when he did so affirm, he of course understood that he was the one who must do the hearkening and the obeying ('*Thou* shalt'). Common worship, therefore, was a dominant factor in keeping the meaning of the sacred story alive as a vitalizing force in community life and as the basis of individual hope and effort. Even the most cursory reader of the Psalms cannot fail to be impressed by this fact: for example, Ps. 106.1–5, in which we see the common shift from community to individual, from praise to responsibility, and from duty to hope:

> *O give thanks unto the Lord, for he is good;*
> *For his grace endureth forever.*
> *Who can recite the mighty acts of the Lord?*
> *Who can show forth all his praise?*
> *Happy are they who keep justice,*
> *He who does right at all times!*
> *Remember me, O Lord, in the favour shown thy people;*

[1] For the precise distribution of the various types of offerings on these occasions see Lev. 23 and Num. 28–29. That covenant renewal ceremonies took place periodically at least during the fall festival at certain periods of the history seems clear from such passages as Deut. 31.9–13; Neh. 8–10 and from numerous other indications as well. The Book of Deuteronomy contains considerable evidence that much of its material was ultimately derived from such a ceremony.

Visit me with thy salvation
That I may see the good of thy chosen,
That I may rejoice in the joy of thy nation,
That I may glory with thine inheritance.

A second illustration of the importance of history in community life and worship is to be seen in the objective nature of confessions and proclamation which ultimately gave form to the sacred literature. Since community was God's work, worship was filled with both confession and proclamation of it. According to Oscar Cullman's study of *The Earliest Christian Confessions*,[1] the two formulæ which were central in the worship of the early Church were: 'Jesus Christ is Lord' (I Cor. 12.3) and 'Jesus is the Son of God' (Acts. 8.37 margin; Heb. 4.14; I John 4.15). Both of these statements it may be noted were derived from what to the New Testament were acts of God. The first refers to the resurrection and exaltation of Christ as the reigning Lord of Creation. The second is the same, though emphasizing by means of a Davidic or royal title drawn from the Old Testament the special relationship existing between God and Christ.[2] When these statements were expanded, the expansion was almost always in the form of additions from what to the Christian were the facts of Jesus' life, death and resurrection (cf. Rom 1.1–3; I Cor. 15.3–7, Phil. 2.6–11).

The substance of the early confessions was derived, of course, from the preaching or kerygma of the early Church.

[1] Translated by J. K. S. Reid, London, 1949.

[2] Cf. II Sam. 7.14; Ps. 2.7. The source of the title 'Son of God' has frequently been debated, but to those who have made a special study of the royal theology of the Jerusalem court, its origin in the Semitic sense can scarcely be in doubt. Later, by means of the birth narratives, it was understood in another sense.

In C. H. Dodd's discussion of this kerygma[1] we observe how it too is centred in the work which God has done and will do in Christ. It is thus an interpretation by inference of the actual life and death of One whose advent was the climax and fulfilment of past history and at the same time the beginning of God's new age. Hence, it is incumbent upon everyone to repent that God may forgive and send his Holy Spirit upon him, for in Christ God has delivered men from sin into life. As Dodd shows, this kerygma is the nerve centre of the New Testament. It is not derived from the Gospels, but the latter are expanded from it by means of a variety of sources of tradition. The Epistles presuppose it, and defend, interpret and apply it. To the Christian community, then, the unity of life, worship and proclamation was nourished by an intensity of conviction about what had happened in Christ's appearance on earth, and about the manner in which this illumined both past and future, so that hope had a substance in divine promise rather than in the natural capacities of man.

The sign and seal of the promise was Christ himself, but he was no isolated phenomenon in history with nothing to illumine his meaning. Behind him was the Scripture, the sacred writings of Israel, which he opened to the Church so that the latter understood them afresh. Early Christian interpretation of the Old Testament involved no comprehensive system of doctrinal meaning and no carefully conceived set of rules for exegesis. It was instead a Spirit-led study in which the God who had directed the events of the chosen nation, was seen to bring them to completion and fulfilment in Christ. The sacred story, thus, was understood to point beyond itself, to prefigure and to lead forward to the ends which God himself had determined. To the early Church the most significant thing in the Old Testament was not simply the

[1] *The Apostolic Preaching and its Developments*, London, 1936.

73

law of God, but the *activity* of God. This activity constituted a redemptive history, the first stage in God's work to usher in his kingdom. The events and personalities in the Old Testament were considered, not as ends in themselves, but as pointing to their fulfilment. They were 'types' in the sense that they were the anticipation and preparation for God's work in Christ.

In proclaiming God's activity in the history of the Chosen People the Jerusalem kerygma characteristically selected a certain part of the history as normative for the meaning of the whole. That was the story from Abraham to David. A clear example of this selection is the brief summary of an address attributed to the Apostle Paul in Acts 13.16ff. It is a typical confession of what God has done, followed by an exhortation based upon the confession. The following are its articles of faith: (1) The God of Israel chose the fathers (Patriarchs); (2) he delivered their progeny with uplifted arm from Egyptian slavery and bare with them in the wilderness; (3) he directed the conquest and divided the land by lot; (4) after the judges, Samuel and the rejected Saul, he raised up David to be their king, as a man after his own heart; (5) of whose seed, according to promise, he raised up a Saviour, Jesus.

It is important to observe that in the Old Testament itself the first three of the above elements were the central articles of confession. Gerhard von Rad has shown that the core of the Hexateuch is a kerygmatic proclamation, a credo, which has been expanded by a great variety of materials from different sources of tradition.[1] The earliest forms of this kerygma are to be found in old cultic confessions (e.g. Deut. 26.5ff.) which describe God's freeing Israel from Egyptian bondage and his gift of an inheritance in which the people are to find rest.

[1] *Das formgeschichtliche Problem des Hexateuchs*, Giessen, 1938; *Das erste Buch Mose: Genesis Kapital 1–12, 9, Das Alte Testament Deutsch*, ed. by V. Herntrich and A. Weiser, Teilband 1, Göttingen, 1948, pp. 7ff.

In the earliest edition and the basic narrative of the Hexateuch (the Yahwist or J narrative) certain expansions of the theme of the old confessions are evident. With the idea of election as central the author has expanded the Patriarchal traditions by collecting stories from various sources and unifying them under the theme of God's promises which lead to subsequent fulfilment. By his edition of the creation stories he has set Israel's election in a world-wide setting as God's answer to the problem of all men (cf. Gen. 12.1–3). By elaborating the Sinai covenant tradition he, together with the Elohist, has presented the conditional nature of the election, God's demand as well as his promise and salvation, the law in the setting of the kerygmatic gospel. The priestly editors have added the cultic traditions so that the means of worship and the conception of the tabernacling God in the community's midst might be preserved.

Here, then, is what God has done, what he has promised, and what he demands as the condition of the fulfilment of promise. The Deuteronomic and Chronicler's histories of the people in their land were both written by inferential application of these presuppositions to subsequent events.[1] To the old kerygma the problem of government brought a new element: the promise to and covenant with David and his dynasty, which subsequently became central in Messianic theology. The prophets made clear the implications of the proclamation to succeeding generations, so that its meaning was seen always to be directly relevant to every historical situation (cf. Isa. 1.2: 'I have nourished and brought up children,

[1] The Deuteronomic history extends from Joshua through II Kings; it is an interpretation of the nation's history which derives its presuppositions from the Book of Deuteronomy. The work of the Chronicler is concerned with the history of Judah and is contained in I and II Chronicles, Ezra and Nehemiah.

but . . .'; Amos 3.2: 'You only have I known; therefore . . .';
Hos. 11.1: 'When Israel was a child, then I loved him . . .').
The psalmists preserve the liturgical response of worshippers
in different situations to God's activity. The wisdom writers
sought to make clear what prudential daily life under 'the fear of
Yahweh' meant, though their lack of the truly kerygmatic perspective shows their close relation to the international sources
of this movement and became the occasion for theological
criticism of much of wisdom's basis (in Job and Ecclesiastes)—
a problem not resolved until the intertestamental period.[1]

It is thus clear that in the Bible we have to do with a
community of a most remarkable and unusual kind. Its
worship, confession, proclamation and sacred literature were
for the most part and centrally dominated by the understanding of God as Lord of history who had created a special
community, revealed to it the manner of its life, provided for it
the means of interpreting events by chosen spokesmen, and by
unmerited acts and promises had given to it hope in the midst of
the tragedies of history. This type of theocentric concentration
sustained the community because attention was on its Lord, on
what he had done and would yet do, and on what he rightfully
claimed from his people. To biblical man, then, the peoples of
the earth who did not acknowledge God's sovereignty, who
had no consciousness of God's role in sustaining community,
or of any responsibility which they bore toward their Creator—
such people could not hope for a future in and through their
social structures, except by God's temporary sufferance. Their
societies and the gods who gave them sanction were man-
made; the promises in them were illusory; in time of trouble
their communities would disintegrate because there was no
power beyond themselves to sustain them.

[1] Cf. J. Coert Rylaarsdam, *Revelation in Jewish Wisdom Literature*,
Chicago, 1946.

B. The Nature of the New Society

Biblical community in both the Old and New Testaments, understanding itself to be a special divine creation, was thus more inclined to think of itself as a people than as an organization. This is as true for the Church of the first and second centuries after Christ as it was for the children of Israel. This Church was the new people of God, the spiritual Israel which was the heir of the promises lost to the Israel after the flesh because of hardness of heart. The Roman world at the time was filled with a variety of cults, secret societies and brotherhoods, designed to give answer to man's religious and social needs. In this respect it was quite similar to the Western world of our day. Yet there was little cohesion among these numerous societies and clubs; none of them created a 'people'. To be sure, most of them had no racial and class barriers; they could win adherents from a cosmopolitan world even as could Christianity. Yet in none of them was there the consciousness of 'Peoplehood' which existed in the Christian community. According to A. D. Nock, 'the Christians had something new—the letters of introduction given to a member of one community about to visit another. The relations and mutual assistance of one congregation to another (as for instance of Rome to Corinth), the formulation of agreed tenets and of an agreed view of their own history. Apart from times of persecution, a poor man must have gained a great sense of security,' for 'he knew that care would be taken of him in and after life, and that he would not be wholly left to his own resources.'[1]

[1] A. D. Nock, *Conversion: the Old and the New in Religion from Alexander the Great to Augustine of Hippo*, London, New York, Toronto, 1933, p. 242. It may be argued that a partial parallel to the biblical conception of 'peoplehood' existed in the Roman Empire,

1. An examination of biblical terminology for the community makes the above point quite clear. The new society thought of itself as the 'people of God', and in using this name a distinction was kept between people and peoples. The people of God were an *'am* (Hebrew; especially in prophetic times) or *laos* (Greek), whereas the people of the world were usually designated by different terms, Hebrew *goi* and Greek *ethnos*. The dominant form of expression was that God chose or took a *laos* (*'am*) from the *ethne*. For example, during the Jerusalem conference over the question of Gentiles Peter described the gift of the Spirit to the Gentiles in the early days of the Church's life. James summed up by saying: 'Symeon has related how God first visited to take from the *ethne* a *laos* for his name' (Acts 15.14).

In the Old Testament the term 'Israel' designated a certain national and political entity, the people who belonged to one nation in which common tradition and ancestry were dominant. Yet in most instances of use religious overtones were involved. Israel was the people of Yahweh, his chosen among the peoples. The earliest forms of the Hexateuchal tradition, before their current written stage and probably antedating the monarchy, are dominated by a conception of Israel or 'all Israel' as 'the people of Yahweh'. A national consciousness existed before it was given political form in the Davidic monarchy;[1] and it was one in which common

with its sense of destiny and with its citizenship, which was increasingly extended to 'barbarians'. Yet such a combination of idealism and patriotism is scarcely a true parallel to biblical conceptions. In any event, we may doubt that it influenced the beliefs of the first century Church to any extent.

[1] See further, Martin Noth, *Geschichte Israels*, Göttingen, 1950, pp. 1–7. It should also be indicated, however, that the use of the term *'am* for Israel as distinct from the use of *goi* for the the pagan nations is much more common in later than in early Israel.

ancestral tradition was coupled with an acknowledgement of God's redemptive activity in which he became the governing Lord of the people. The factors of race, blood and genealogy would never in themselves have created Israel as we meet her on the pages of the Old Testament. For this reason, it was possible in prophetic times for a tension to exist between national Israel and faithful Israel, of which we hear as early as the time of Elijah (I Kings 19.18), and between the nation and its 'remnant', so prominent in Isaiah. This tension continued in the New Testament where we hear of the 'little flock' (Luke 12.32) of a 'remnant, chosen by grace' (Rom. 11.5), of the true Israel which is the Israel after the Spirit as distinct from the Israel after the flesh (cf. Rom. 9.6ff), of the 'Israel of God' which is a new creation (Gal. 6.15–16).[1]

In biblical faith, therefore, when God created the new community, whether that of the Old or of the New Testament, he created a people. This consciousness of being a people distinguished the community from those guilds, clubs and religious societies which were as typical of the Roman world as they are of ours. While the conception of peoplehood originated in the factors of nationality and race in the Old Testament, it cannot be defined by them in its biblical sense. Since it was God who brought the people into being and who entered into 'controversy' with them that they might become his faithful community, nation and race became inadequate as a means of defining its extent. In the Old Testament the prophets pointed to the true Israel *within* the nation, whereas in the New Testament by a logical extension Israel became the 'seed of Abraham' by faith rather than by heredity.

2. A second factor which distinguishes the biblical 'people' from an organization is to be found in the secondary and

[1] See further, e.g. R. Newton Flew, *Jesus and His Church*, New York, 1938, pp. 139ff.

ancillary role of organization within the community. In the ancient polytheistic world political kingship and temple were the very foundation and life of the social structure.[1] Yet in Israel, despite all attempts of kings and priests to achieve a similar status, neither kingship nor temple possessed the sanctity or the permanence which would enable them to be adequate symbols of the nation's inner life. Israel as the people of God existed before either of them came into being and subsequently continued to exist without them. Israel's golden age was understood to be the era of David and Solomon in the tenth century B.C., but the prophets did not appeal to it as the model for community life. Instead they pointed to the wilderness period when the bond between people and Deity was particularly close.

In the New Testament the new community was astonishingly free of institutionalism and fixed organization. While, to be sure, a framework was provided by its original position within Judaism, this framework was not a rigid structure. Its primary unity was derived from other sources which made it a people instead of another guild or cult among many similar. A number of terms were used which indicate this fact: e.g. 'family of Christ', 'household of faith', the 'New Covenant', 'assembly', 'synagogue', 'fellowship', 'body of Christ', 'bride of Christ', the 'little flock', a vine with its branches, *ecclesia* (church), etc. Several of these terms indicate the special relationship existing between the people and Christ which reveals the inner basis of community life. For example, the Johannine figure of the vine (John 15.1–8): Christ is the vine; the individuals of the community are the branches; and God is the vine-dresser. The branches bear the fruit, but they are able to do so only because they remain in the vine

[1] See especially, Henri Frankfort, *Kingship and the Gods*, Chicago, 1948.

without which they are nothing. The worthless branches are cut away and burned by the Father, and the rest are pruned that they may bear more fruit. In this way the organism remains healthy and productive, and the method by which the Vine-Dresser is glorified is 'that you bear much fruit, and so prove to be my disciples' (v. 8).

The Pauline figure of the body of Christ (*soma Christou*) is equally expressive. As has been realized in recent years, the term 'body' is here used in a Hebraic, rather than Hellenic, sense. It is not something in which the mind or spirit is imprisoned, but it is the total person as a living organism.[1] Hence the body of Christ is Christ himself. To speak of the new community as Christ's body is to emphasize the fact that it is a living, unified organism by means of the principle of corporate personality so common in the Semitic world. Christ is the community, and the community is 'in Christ'. This manner of speaking is anticipated in the Gospels where the disciples are identified with Christ: e.g. 'he who receives you receives me' (Matt. 10.40; cf. Mark 9.37; Luke 10.16). It is also implicit in the ancient identification of a king with his subjects, of a patriarchal father with his family, of the Servant in Second Isaiah with his people. By means of the term 'body' the Apostle Paul is able to express the nature of the new society as a vital organism in the strongest possible manner. Individual members with their variety of talents can be likened to the members of a body, so that 'There are many parts, yet one body' (I Cor. 12.20). In the life of the body Christ can be conceived as the head, 'from the whole body, nourished and knit together through its joints and ligaments,

[1] See Clarence T. Craig, 'Soma Christou', *The Joy of Study* (ed. by Sherman E. Johnson), New York, 1951, pp. 73–85, with references there cited; and John A. T. Robinson, *The Body: A Study in Pauline Theology*, London and Chicago, 1952.

grows with a growth that is from God' (Col. 2.19; cf. Eph. 4.16).

Other New Testament figures, such as the 'family of Christ', the 'household of faith', and the 'fellowship', all point to the same conception: namely that the new community in Christ is a people knit together, not primarily by human structures of organization, but instead by an inner mutuality of spirit provided by God in Christ. Behind such terms lies the conception of a people bound together in covenant with its Lord which arose in the Old Testament. The covenant converted a group of families and individuals into a 'household' or fellowship (Eph. 2.11–22). The community conceived as the 'Bride of Christ' (Rev. 21.9; cf. Eph. 5.31–32) has the same background, a figure probably related to the allegorical interpretation of the Song of Songs and to Hosea's use of the marriage bond to signify the covenant relationship between God and Israel, one which the latter had broken. Inasmuch as God had chosen one group from among the nations and formed it into a people (*laos*), there existed between him and his people a close tie to which reference is made by a variety of languages in both Testaments. The dominant language in the Old Testament was derived from the conception of covenant, though the term itself is not used with equal frequency by the various writers.[1]

Covenant as a name for the bond between God and Israel held within it a political anthropomorphism in which God appeared as Lord or King and the people as his 'servants' or subjects. The Lord did not force the people into this relationship; he offered it to them as a gracious act and promised them

[1] It is most frequent in the literature of the Deuteronomist, Priestly writers and Chronicler and less so in the Psalms. The actual term is not used so often in the prophets. In the Wisdom literature because of the wise man's special interests the kerygmatic message centred in history, election and covenant is almost entirely lacking.

his leadership, justice and salvation. When the people accepted this offer, they in turn promised to 'obey' and to 'serve' their ruler. He provided their government; they were to 'hearken' and to be 'obedient' to His will. The terms 'Judge', 'Saviour', and 'Shepherd', as used of God, were derived from the same background of kingship and referred to the various functions of the rule. This ruler-servant terminology was the basic language of Israelite faith, and was the source of the legal terms so commonly used in the religious vocabulary. Thus, though the prophets do not make large use of the term 'covenant', they presuppose the binding nature of a compact which would be depicted in legal terms, and they could proclaim God's controversy (i.e. legal case) against his chosen nation for its rebellion against his Lordship (e.g. Isa. 1.2; Jer. 2.1–13; Hos. 4.1–3; Micah 6.1–5).

In this light it is quite clear that the society of Israel cannot be viewed as one human organization among others in which common ancestral and cultural roots, together with human structures of power and authority, were the chief characterizing features. To be Israel meant to be a people existing in a special contractual relationship with God the Lord. This relationship of common loyalty, in which loving and free-hearted obedience to the Ruler meant also the service and loving consideration of all other members of the community, created a 'fellowship', a 'household of faith', a 'family'. And the community of the New Testament, accepting the Lordship of the risen Christ, was the successor and heir of this conception. The Johannine figure of the vine and the Pauline description of the body make this quite clear, as also does the use of the term 'New Covenant'.

The biblical community, therefore, could be conceived as an assembly in fellowship with God and with one another. It was a gathered people, a congregation before its Lord, one which existed in and by its Head. The Greek name *ekklesia* (church) as used for the community must accordingly be defined, neither by its etymology nor by its meaning in non-biblical Greek, but by its biblical content.[1] It was the word adopted by the Septuagint translators as the usual rendering for the Hebrew *qahal*, and both meant simply the congregation of God's people.[2]

3. Inasmuch as the biblical community thought of itself as a people, tied to its Lord by a formal bond which was sanctioned by love, trust and inner assent, the conduct of life and of history was believed to be under the Lord's direct governance. The kingship of Christ in the New Testament and of God himself over Israel was exercised from the heavenly throne. Yet it was known to be nonetheless effective because God ruled by chosen human media and by direct communication through his heavenly messengers (angels), his word (and wisdom), and his Spirit. This meant that all organization and government were conceived to be of divine institution and sanction, or else they were useless, unprofitable, even sinful. This also meant that any institution which apparently had received a permanent blessing could find itself in condemnation and deprived of blessing when it failed to fulfil its God-given task. The conception of a direct heavenly rule meant the

[1] See further, e.g. George Johnson, *The Doctrine of the Church in the New Testament*, Cambridge, 1943, pp. 35–45. Contrast in part Karl Ludwig Schmidt in G. Kittel, *Theologisches Wörterbuch zum Neuen Testament*, Vol. III, p. 516, cf. 534 (tr. by J. R. Coates, under the title, *The Church*, London, 1950, p. 24; cf. pp. 57ff.). Common words of great age and usage can rarely be defined adequately by etymology.

[2] In the Old Testament two terms, *'edah* and *qahal*, are used synonymously for the community. The usual translation of the first is *synagoge*, though other terms are used and considerable mixture occurs. *'Edah* is the term preferred by the Priestly writers, while the Deuteronomist and Chronicle prefer *qahal*.

subjection of all human organization to it, and every promise and blessing given by God was contingent on obedient loyalty. Saul was chosen; then rejected. The kingdom was established; then destroyed. The cultus traced its origin to the revelation on Sinai; yet the divine Word by both prophet and apostle proclaimed that God now despised it or that it held no permanent status in his plans. Among the terrible words which Ezekiel heard from God were two which especially shocked him. One was the command to eat unclean food (4.13–14) and the other was the divine order to 'defile the house' (Temple, 9.7). Pious sensibilities, trained in a tradition which once had received God's sanction, meant more to man than to God. The latter by his rule could shock and dismay; institutionalism and the pious feelings connected with it received no permanent 'Yea' from the heavenly throne.

In pre-monarchial Israel God's leadership of the people was believed to have been exercised charismatically. That is, human leaders empowered by God's Spirit were chosen and sent by God to perform specific tasks. Joshua was no son of Moses, but one whom God had selected and empowered to lead the conquest. After the completion of the main part of that task, no head of the whole people was conceived necessary. God ruled directly, and in times of crisis empowered individuals to deal with the specific issue of the moment, but no more. Neither the attempts of Abimelek, nor those of the sons of Eli or of Samuel, to perpetuate a political leadership in one family were successful. Gideon's affirmation to those who wished to turn his temporary, charismatic office into a monarchy preserve the ideology of the period: 'I will not rule over you, and my son will not rule over you; the Lord will rule over you' (Judg. 8.23).

Yet David was the last of the truly charismatic figures in political life. Dynastic succession gave permanence and stability to the government in Jerusalem, and God's rule was now conceived to operate through a chosen king with whose dynasty he had made an everlasting covenant. The priestly office was regulated and adjusted to political authority. Institutionalism replaced the freer, Spirit-led, tribal association (or amphictyony) of the earlier time. Yet the God of Israel was of such a nature that the exercise of his Lordship could never be confined or forced to operate within institutions alone. The office of prophecy was the place where the ideal of charisma remained supreme.[1] The Prophet was the herald of the Divine King; he was one sent to speak a Word which was not his own. His 'Thus saith the Lord' had an authority above all other human voices and authorities. He was chosen and empowered by God, and no human rite of ordination or induction into office was fitting or desirable. His was an office regulated not by the consent of those whom he was to address, but solely by God. The freedom from human institutionalism was prophecy's greatest strength in Israel's theocracy, though it was also its greatest danger. In the course of time the country was overrun with prophets, most of whom, as Jeremiah put it, got their messages from themselves and the people, rather than from God (Jer. 23.30: 'Behold, I am against the prophets, saith the Lord, that steal my words every one from his neighbour!'). Hence prophecy promptly turned against prophecy, and men like Micaiah, Amos and Jeremiah dissociated themselves from those whose vocation was increasingly institutionalized. The freedom permitted by the conception of charisma was greatly abused, but without it the great prophets would never have arisen and the

[1] It is not improbable that, after the division of the kingdom, North Israel attempted to return to the charismatic ideal of political leadership, though without success. See e.g. Martin Noth, *Geschichte Israels*, Göttingen, 1950, pp. 198ff.

Israelite community as a people of God would not have survived the destruction of life, property and political institutions.

It is important to observe that in prophetic eschatology the consummation of the kingdom of God is to be marked by a great revival of charismatic happenings. Both leaders and people will be Spirit-filled and Spirit-empowered on a scale hitherto unknown, though foreshadowed in the pre-monarchial age. A dominant element in Scriptural typology is the conception of the end as the re-establishment and fulfilment of the beginning, while at the same time it inaugurates the new age. For the prophets the charismatic period of Israel's history was its typical age, and the end-time would see its fulfilment (e.g. Isa. 11.2, 42.1, 44.3; Ezek. 36.27, 37.14; Joel 2.28–9; Zech. 4.6).

It is against this background that we comprehend the New Testament's absorption with the work of the Holy Spirit. The new age in Christ is one in which the people of God are led, purified, empowered and enlightened by the Spirit. For this reason there is no detailed interest in institutionalism of and for itself. It has often been affirmed that the history of the Church during the late first and second centuries of our era is marked by an increasing institutionalism, with its concern for the details of rules and rites and with a corresponding diminution of interest in the relation of Church and Holy Spirit. The sub-Apostolic thinkers actually had no doctrine of the Spirit at all. Yet the primitive Church was almost exclusively a charismatic community, and 'for Paul the Ecclesia was essentially an almost world-wide fellowship of the Spirit, taking form and name in local congregations, cells in the one Body of the exalted Christ.'[1] As in pre-monarchial Israel and in later prophecy leadership was not created by the

[1] George Johnson, op. cit., p. 111: see also R. Newton Flew, op. cit., Chap. 6 and pp. 259ff.

community. It was given to the Church by the glorified Lord through the work of the Spirit. Word and Spirit had created the community, and the various ministries in the Church were dominantly charismatic. Individuals were understood to have been marked out for this or that special function by the divers gifts (*charismata*) accorded them. To be sure, the freedom accorded the Spirit-led community could be abused, even as it was in Israel. The problem of false prophecy and speaking with tongues was evidently very real, so that we read exhortations to 'test the spirits whether they are of God' (I John 4.1) and to make sure of the edifying nature of prophecy (I Cor. 14). Yet the Lordship of Christ over the Church was mediated through the Spirit's work, and it was confidently believed that the affirmation of Lordship exercised in this manner was not an ideal or ethereal conception but the most relevant and practical affirmation that could be made. Of course, the work of the Spirit was not in an organizational vacuum. Affairs were regularized and done in order. Biblical community, however, was conceived primarily as an organism rather than as an organization, and the Divine direction of community life by Word and Spirit could not be circumscribed by institutions which at best had but a temporal, and usually temporary function.

C. INDIVIDUAL AND COMMUNITY

1. The Bible's concentration upon the new community which God had brought into being as a people had as its correlate the implication that the individual member of the community will and must be a new creature. Biblical society was so intensely self-conscious of its radical difference from other societies that the individual had constantly before him the conception of two different ways of life. Between them

he had to make a conscious choice. In other words, entrance into the Church of Christ from pagan society was by way of conversion.

Baptism as an entrance rite signified one's engagement to be the Lord's through repentance and faith, purification from sin and consecration to the new life. John's baptism was preceded and accompanied by 'repentance unto remission of sins' (Mark 1.4). It was, however, administered largely to those of the faith who wished to be prepared for entrance into the community of the New Age. The baptism of the latter, John claimed, would not be simply by water but by the Holy Spirit (Mark 1.8). Since the New Testament community was empowered and led by the Spirit, entrance into it was accompanied by the gift of the Spirit. Hence a new and very different life was envisaged by the individual who entered the fellowship. Baptism was the sign and seal of a completely new existence (e.g. Acts 2.38).

The Jewish antecedents of Christian baptism evidently had a similar significance. While our evidence for proselyte baptism is later than the New Testament period, it is believed to testify to far older practice. There is evidence also that the rite may have been the means of entrance into certain of the Jewish Sects. In any event, the earliest witness to its existence outside the New Testament is now to be found in the literature of the Covenanters. This sect, probably of pre-Christian origin, believed itself to be the true people of God over against the dominant parties in Jerusalem thought to be apostate to the covenant. The semi-monastic life of the Covenanters was governed by the strictest discipline and by constant study of the law. Before an outsider could obtain full membership in the group, he had to undergo a training period, deeply repent of his former life, submit himself entirely to the revealed law, that his flesh 'be cleansed so that he may purify himself with water for impurity and sanctify himself with rippling water'. Perverse men 'who walk in the way of wickedness . . . are not reckoned in His covenant', and they 'may not enter into water to [be permitted to] touch the Purity of the holy men, for they will not be cleansed unless they have turned from their wickedness'.[1] The reference here to the rite of cleansing water cannot be assumed to be a simple magical ceremony, because the agent of purification is expressly said to be God through his Holy Spirit, a 'Spirit disposed toward Unity in His truth', which cleanses one of 'the spirit of impurity' and gives one an understanding of heavenly counsels.[2]

The rite of entrance in Jewish and Christian communities thus signifies the necessity of a radical choice to be made by the individual member. The latter was joining a people who were conscious of their differences, determined to be faithful to their Divine calling, and bearing witness to a destiny which fulfilled the past and present. He thus underwent conversion, an experience which has been defined as 'the re-orientation of the soul of an individual, his deliberate turning from indifference or from an earlier form of piety to another, a

[1] See William H. Brownlee, 'The Dead Sea Manual of Discipline', *Bulletin of the American Schools of Oriental Research*, *Supplementary Studies*, Nos. 10–12, New Haven, 1951, Col. iii, lines 6–9; Col. v, lines 13–14. This early witness to baptism seems not to have received treatment in the discussion of the subject thus far.

[2] *Ibid.*, Col. iii, lines 7–8; Col. iv, lines 21–2. The fact that baptism was preceded by repentance among the Covenanters gives further support to those who have argued the same for the baptism of John. On the latter, see further Josephus, *Antiquities*, Book XVIII.5.2; Carl H. Kraeling, *John the Baptist*, New York, 1951, pp. 75ff.; and the discussion of J. R. Mantey and Ralph Marcus in *Journal of Biblical Literature*, Vol. LXX, 1951, pp. 45ff., 129f., 309ff.; Vol. LXXI, 1952, pp. 43f.

turning which implies a consciousness that a great change is involved, that the old was wrong and the new right.'[1] Moreover, in the New Testament community the individual who had put off the old man and put on the new was characterized by Spirit-possession, so that the gifts and fruits of the Spirit were constantly held before him (e.g. Rom. 12; I Cor. 12–14). He lived in a 'household of faith', the 'family of Christ' who had died for him, whom he must follow and imitate, and to whom he must be obedient even, if necessary, unto death. Nothing in life or death need cause him fear or panic, for God who had raised and exalted Jesus from the death of the Cross could not be defeated by the rebellious powers of this world. As A. D. Nock has pointed out, this type of conversion is something very different from membership in a polytheistic religion, which he characterizes by the word 'adherence', and from the new life promised by the mystery cults of the Roman Empire. The latter were developments from polytheism in which the magical element remained central. The salvation promised by Orphism, for example, was a blessedness 'secured by a rite in which the initiate went through a symbolic anticipation of what was to take place hereafter; it was a piece of sympathetic magic which ensured safety by a simulation here and now. Death and rebirth have this meaning and no other . . . the rites were actions efficient in themselves as rites and not as the expression of a theology and of a world-order sharply contrasted with those in which the neophyte had previously moved.'[2]

In the Old Testament perhaps the first clearly recorded instance of conversion is that of Saul, who when anointed by Samuel was empowered by the Spirit so that it is said: 'God gave him another heart' (I Sam. 10.9). Because of the nationalistic basis of the society, however, the situation in Israel was

[1] A. D. Nock, op. cit., p. 7.   [2] Ibid., pp. 12–13.

91

obviously quite different from what it was in Judaism and Christianity. To be an Israelite was to be a member of the people of God because the covenant vows taken by the fathers, and periodically renewed at various services, were held binding upon the whole community. Yet two facts in particular may be stressed as furnishing the soil in which later developments were already planted.

One of these facts is the incipient missionary emphasis in Old Testament faith. This is to be seen in the belief that through Israel as agent God was to bring all peoples under his sovereignty, a belief expressed in various ways by prophetic eschatology and the Book of Jonah, though present as early as the Yahwist writer in the Hexateuch (cf. Gen. 12.3). Furthermore, it is necessary to assume missionary activity in the pre-monarchial period in order to explain how 'all Israel' came into being under a single national tradition. Various groups which had not participated in the Exodus and who had not been at Sinai nevertheless adopted these events as the normative expression of faith and teaching by covenant ceremonies such as that recorded in Josh. 24. Among these groups were several clans who could claim no common geneology in the fathers.[1] Client strangers and sojourners who lived within the Israelite community were provided for in the law so that they could share all the privileges of community life and worship, if they chose, without discrimination. From this point it was but a step to the later Jewish proselyte movement carried on after the dispersion of the national community.

A second and perhaps even more important factor was the

[1] Cf. also the mention of the 'mixed multitude' or 'rabble' which left Egypt under Moses (Num. 11.4). The Hivite covenant with Israel was of course an act of political expediency rather than of religious conviction (Josh. 9).

preaching of the prophets. Walter Eichrodt[1] has described the prophetic attack upon all established institutions as a 'resolute defence against all those social movements in religion which are reared like isolating walls around the individual, robbing him of the sense of being set face to face with God, and forcing him down into the mass'. He continues:

'The cry *shubu*—"Turn!"—sounds through this whole period as one of the basic words of the prophetic proclamation, and this asks of the individual a conscious decision against the constraint of the collective will and against the pressure of a cultural development encouraged by the whole external situation. In the struggle against the reduction of religion to a mass affair by means of a refined exercise of the cult, the watch-cry was coined, "Not sacrifice, but obedience!"[2] and here again the individual is torn from his comfortable position in the religious life of the community and summoned to use his own judgment and make his own decisive contribution. Most remarkable in this connexion are the new form and forceful concentration of the relation with God, which had hitherto simply been described as the fear of God, and is now expressed in words like faith, love, thankfulness, and knowledge of God, which are filled with spiritual tension. For this new way of describing the individual's right attitude to his God not only expresses that bowing before the overwhelming majesty of the holy God, which was proclaimed by the prophets with unheard-of passion; but the strongest possible emphasis falls upon the spiritual initiative of the individual, which is no purely

[1] *Man in the Old Testament* (tr. by K. and R. Gregor Smith), London and Chicago, 1951, pp. 20–1. In German, *Das Menschenverständnis des Alten Testaments*, Basel, 1944, pp. 18–20.

[2] I Sam. 15.22; Amos 5.21–24; Hos. 6.6; Isa. 1.1–11; Jer. 7.21–23.

passive abandonment but demands a conscious grasp of the newly offered reality of life.'

This type of prophetic emphasis on the independence of the individual had dire consequences for the old national unity which had already been deeply compromised by religious syncretism and social cleavage. Yet the prophets never hesitated in making a decision for the spiritual obligation and independence of the individual and against a compromised national structure, loyalty to which promised security. The content of God's will in the covenant was 'Obey my voice' (Jer. 7.21–23; 11.7); and this was a call to commitment and daily decision in obedience to the Lord of history. It implied a freedom, a theocentricity and a conscious choice which were excluded from every interpretation of the covenant as a legal system, from that popular patriotism which claimed the Divine blessing of peace when there was no peace, and from the cowardice of those who blamed all trouble upon the fathers who had eaten sour grapes (Jer. 31.29; Lam. 5.7; Ezek. 18.2). To exist as a community of God's people meant to the prophets that Israel's citizens must be a responsible people, impelled by their commitment to make individual decisions for what was right before the community's Lord.

2. The biblical emphasis upon the inner re-orientation of the individual, upon his deliberate turning from his former ways in response to the challenge, 'Choose you this day', was always a disturbing factor which violated the normal man's integration within state and cult. It is no accident that neither king nor temple was able permanently to achieve the absolutism and sanction which they possessed in the contemporary paganisms.[1] They were unable to maintain themselves as the primary means whereby nature, society and the divine

[1] Cf., e.g. Henri Frankfort, *Kingship and the Gods*, Chicago, 1948.

94

could be integrated within one another. Institutional security was no surrogate for the direct responsibility which man the individual had to his Lord. Within biblical faith a value seems to have been placed upon individual decision and upon direct relationship of responsibility to the divine King, one which could not be transferred to, or be replaced by, collective or institutional responsibility. The great 'calls' or conversions recorded in the Bible were highly personal experiences: yet with the possible exception of that of Saul they were not focused upon the experience as such but instead upon commitment to a specific historical vocation. By them the powers of the individual for responsible action were given focus. Those called stood alone before the task laid upon them, sustained solely by the consciousness of God's directing power behind them, wherein lay their security. Integration was not with the world but with the God whose call had brought a spiritual tension between what is and what will be.

The Divine Lordship over the community thus called for an individual loyalty which took precedence over all other loyalties and implied a 'glory and honour' placed by God on the individual (Ps. 8). Israel's view of the dignity accorded man at the creation is a derivative, an inference, from the knowledge of the responsibility placed upon him by God. As One who offers himself for communion, God 'emerges from his hiddenness into a morally positive relation with his creature, in which he shows him his special place and task in the world. As a creature man is ranged with all other creatures, but now, as the one whom God's Word meets, he comes to God's side and confronts the rest of creation.'[1] Nature now loses its dark mystery together with its gods, its myths and its magic, so that man is no longer bound to its uncanny, instinctive life, as was the case in polytheism. He is liberated to the

[1] Walter Eichrodt, op. cit., p. 30 (English; in the German ed. p. 29).

head of creation, ranged by the side of the Creator in the acceptance of a work which accords with Divine purpose. His commission to work is a blessing (Gen. 1.28) for it contains his goal. History and nature are joined in the Creator, and man as creature is to play his role in the fulfilment of the Divine purpose in creation.

In the New Testament the same presuppositions present in the Old Testament concerning the responsible individual are retained, though with heightened emphasis upon the weakening which sin has brought to the Divine likeness (*imago Dei*) in man. Yet the first man whom God created in his own image furnished the early Church with a 'type' which Christ fulfilled and through Christ is imparted to those who are 'in him'. Christ as 'the image of the invisible God' (Col. 1.15; cf. II Cor. 4.4.) is the second Adam, who instead of bringing death, brings life. 'When Christ who is our life appears, then you also will appear with him in glory' (Col. 3.4). To be in him is to possess a new nature, 'renewed in knowledge after the image of its Creator' (Col. 3.10), 'conformed to the image of his Son' (Rom. 8.29), bearing 'the image of the man of heaven' (I Cor. 15.49), 'being changed into his likeness from one degree of glory to another for this comes from the Lord who is Spirit' (II Cor. 3.18). Hence the thought of the New Testament concentrates upon the restoration of man to full stature that we may be 'heirs of God and fellow heirs with Christ' (Rom. 8.17). In Christ God's intention for man is realized.

3. Yet the new and responsible individual who is created by God in Christ is not liberated from community in such a manner as would enable us to speak of biblical faith as creating a true individualism over against all collectivism. Man is here liberated from a false to a true community, and for that reason his first steps in the right direction are to be discovered

in conversion. While in modern times we see a rediscovery of community which enslaves man, so that collectivism and individualism appear as opposing concepts, the biblical concentration of attention on God's formation of a people is of such a nature that man, the individual, emerges in society in a manner hitherto unknown. The biblical story must not be interpreted as the progressive emancipation of the individual, but instead as God's action in history to create a community in which the responsible individual finds his true being.

The early Christian community after Calvary, Easter and Pentecost lived as a *koinonia*, a fellowship in a common life, under the leadership of the invisible Lord whose spirit 'tabernacled in' and possessed the whole community. The risen and exalted Lord was closer now to the members of the new society than he had ever been in life. Their relationship to one another was determined by their relationship to him. The Golden Rule was silently revised to mean: 'Do unto others as Jesus has done unto you. Love them as he has loved you, hope and sacrifice for your brothers as he has hoped and sacrificed for you, mediate to them the redemptive grace he mediated to you.'[1] Above all the individual was to *follow* his Lord, and the latter's own life on earth was the model and command. Such a community, filled with tremendous enthusiasm and astonishing boldness, at one point even holding many possessions in common, was able to unite individuality within a common allegiance and common purpose. 'One might suppose that all individuality would be swallowed up in this tremendous outburst of collectivism; but such is not the case. The favourite Pauline image for the Christian fellowship (I Cor. 12; Eph. 4), is a body with many organs, each with gifts and functions of its own, different in

[1] So Walter Marshall Horton, 'The Christian Community: Its Lord and Its Fellowship', *Interpretation*, Vol. IV, 1950, p. 392.

operation though equal in honour. In this remarkable capacity of the Christian fellowship to combine individuality with collectivism, freedom of the parts with unity of the whole, lies the great contribution of Christianity to the solution of ethical problems. Nothing could be more relevant to the ethical problems of the world today—split into warring blocks by the opposite attractions of individualism and collectivism—than the actual structure of the early Church, quite apart from its formal ethical teachings.'[1]

As pointed out in Chapter I, the soil in which this conception of community was planted is to be found in the Old Testament. The covenant between God and Israel was the formal expression of community structure which released the individual for a new freedom within a new society. God was no longer remote, but nearer to his people than any other God known hitherto (Deut. 4.7). The Apostle Paul stated Israel's view as his own by a free rendering of a number of Old Testament verses: 'As God hath said: "I will dwell in them, and walk in them; and I will be their God, and they shall be my people. Wherefore come out from among them, and be ye separate," said the Lord, "and touch not the unclean thing; and I will receive you, and will be a Father unto you, and ye shall be my sons and daughters"' (II Cor. 6.16–18). The 'peace', the well-being and harmony of the community was God's blessing to an obedient people. They were to obey him because they loved him (Deut. 6.4ff.), because he had drawn them to himself by his extraordinary acts of grace; and this obedience meant that they were to be holy as he was holy, righteous as he was righteous, reflecting in their love of the neighbour and sojourner his love for them (cf. especially Deut. 10.12–22).

The individual found his life purpose and his true being in

[1] Ibid., pp. 395–6.

this dedicated, obedient, joyous, worshipping community. He was not oppressed by the collective structure, but was found in it, and heard himself singled out as the one to whom God's 'Thou shalt' was addressed. God was the beloved and revered Sovereign of the people, individually, severally and totally. He was no 'respecter of persons'; the privileged few could not conceive of themselves as having more immediate access to his favour. Indeed, to one class alone is he represented as showing partiality, and that is to the poor, whose weakness made them the easy prey of the strong. Hence even the poorest of society's unimportant ones were dignified by the divine vindicator who specifically gave them assurance of direct access to his ear (Exod. 22.23, 27).

The biblical balance between the responsible society and the responsible individual was made possible only because of the unqualified theocentricity of the faith. God himself did and demanded what for man on his own resources is impossible, and absolute loyalty to him took precedence over all other loyalties. As the history of Israel so clearly shows, any weakening of loyalty to God destroyed the people of God as an organism. In the period of the Judges, on the one hand, when idolatry flourished and the amphictyonic solidarity was weakened, the historian pictures a virtual anarchy, 'when every man did what was right in his own eyes' (Judg. 21.25). During the period of the monarchy, on the other hand, the sense of individual responsibility to God was transferred to and subsumed in community conformity, in the collective will, and the nature of the latter was guided very largely by state and temple. Hence the individual's need of personal and responsible decision was weakened, with the result that a legalism based upon the letter of the law flourished with a complete perversion of the law's spirit and intention. At the same time, the will of God and the wills of king and priest were so completely identified in the collective will that God became more the follower than the active Sovereign, the One who existed to help and fulfil rather than to lead. In such a perversion Israelite society became simply another national community. For this reason, the repeated reforms and the prophetic call focussed primary attention on the wilderness period, rather than on the Davidic-Solomonic age, for God then ruled directly and demanded a collective responsibility unmediated by king and temple.

One way of conceiving the biblical doctrine of individual and community is to understand the nature of historical purpose as a series of interlaced or intersecting arches. The purpose of God over-arches all of time. This purpose is being accomplished by means of his election of a people. The time of this people is that needed to fulfil its election, its purpose is a portion of the Divine purpose; its arch is within and organically related to that of God, while at the same time it over-arches the time alloted to each individual of the community. Individuals likewise have their election; but it is one within the temporal arch given the community. The time, the purpose, the task (i.e. the arch) of each person thus forms a part of the community purpose which overarches all components within it. At the same time, however, the individual arches are each unique, separate and structurally important, not only because they are vital components of the larger community arch, but because by a mystery of the Architect they too are tied into, organically related, to the larger span of God. While the value of any figure is limited, this one may in part show the complexity of the biblical organism, where community election is primary and a portion of divine purpose, and where within the community election each individual finds his role. Yet the individual election is likewise divinely given and divinely related; it indicates man's social nature and community calling but it also signalizes man's individual responsibility before God. The people of God and the man of God thus find their status under God in an organism of considerable complexity.

It remains to be said however, that such a society was in the Bible a revealed order, never completely actualized but always existing as the judge of the existing orders. The 'individualism' of the prophets was a divine repudiation of the existing collectivism. It was a call to stand for the revealed order and to accept isolation as the divine judgment fell upon the nation. Yet this isolation had no permanent status. It was instead a necessary condition, imposed temporarily, as God laboured to create a faithful people. In this case the individual arch supported the remnant of the people's arch which God was repairing and reconstituting.

D. The Common Life of the New Society

Community life among the people of God was not rooted in a natural law believed to have been written into the constitution of the created world, nor was it a derivative from the state. Instead, common life was based upon the understanding of the righteousness of God. This righteousness had brought the community into being, and bound its members to its Giver with ties of gratitude, trust and devotion. Ethics was thus an obedience rooted in devotion, and neighbourly dealings were to be a response to the love which first loved the chosen. The personal attachment to the community's Lord transformed the meaning and function of law and at the same time did that which no law could ever do. It made true community life possible on a basis other than legalism, distributive justice, or juridical calculation of what is the just due of every man according to his social status.

1. For the early Christian community life was created and sustained in the acknowledgment that 'Jesus Christ is Lord, to the glory of God the Father' (Phil. 2.11). Christ is the righteousness of God. He had no interest in being equal with God, but emptied himself by becoming obedient unto death. The Christian who acknowledges Christ's Lordship must possess the same mind and the same obedience, with the result that in love he will act without strife or vainglory, looking not only to his own affairs, but in humility being concerned primarily with the lot of others. The 'encouragement in Christ', the 'incentive of love', and 'participation in the Spirit' bring Christians together, 'of the same mind, having the same love, being in full accord' (Phil. 2.2). Acknowledgment of Christ's Lordship is thus not an intellectual assent to a dogmatic proposition, but an active participation in the 'mind of Christ' which results in community. It leads to an ethic which cannot be frozen into a system of law or justice because it is a free self-giving to those in need. This does not mean that it is antinomian, but that it goes beyond all law in order to make the community of God's people possible. To confess Christ is thus the most relevant political and social statement that one can make, not in the sense that it tells the Christian precisely how to act in a secular society, but that it provides the inner ground of all action and involves a participation in community living as a vocation to which one is called. Hence the Christian is enjoined: 'Work out your own salvation with fear and trembling, for it is God who works in you both to will and to do for his good pleasure' (Phil. 2.12–13). In so doing one will possess, not a righteousness of law, but a righteousness that is 'through faith in Christ, the righteousness from God that depends on faith' (Phil. 3.9).

This viewpoint, as is well known, led to a paradoxical

position with regard to law. On the one hand, the law is of God, it is his will laid before us; Jesus did not annul it; and the Epistles, after theological exposition, generally conclude with ethical exhortations. Hence, in some manner, Gospel and law appear to be joined together. On the other hand, the freedom of Jesus in dealing with questions of law, and the liberty in Christ as enjoined by the Apostle Paul, would appear to set the law aside as the important focus of the Christian's attention.

To understand this paradox we must see its background and rootage in the Old Testament. There the *debarim* or 'words' of God are understood to be the Ten Commandments (Exod. 20.1; Deut. 4.12–13; 5.22ff.). These belong to a kind of legal formulation known as apodictic law, the type addressed by the Divine Ruler to his people as a direct command. Its presupposition is the necessity of absolute obedience, and its purpose is to lay before the people God's absolute will as the norm to which the society must adhere. The other type of law in the Old Testament is the casuistic or case law, called 'the statutes and ordinances' (Exod. 21.1; Deut. 4.14), which was considered to have been mediated to Israel by Moses. It is the law which bears so many resemblances to other law codes of the ancient Near East. Its typical formulation is impersonal; it begins with an 'if' clause which defines the case and concludes in the main clause with a description of the penalty.[1] This law arose from legal decisions in specific cases which were to act as guides or precedents (cf. Exod. 18). Its purpose was not to serve as statutory law with power to coerce. It was flexible and kept up to date in order to balance conflicting interests. Its codification was in order to unify the people, to do away with many local differences, so that there might be for the one people under God one law and one set of

[1] See A. Alt, *Die Ursprünge des israelitischen Rechts*, Leipzig, 1934.

ordinances. Neither the Israelite Book of the Covenant (Exod. 21–23) nor the earlier Hammurabi Code were law as we customarily think of it. They were common law, descriptions of justice or legal procedure, written down for information. Hence the general Hebrew word for law, *torah*, meant 'teaching, instruction'. The whole status of law changed, however, beginning in the time of Josiah and continuing through the Post-Exilic period into Judaism, when the attempt was made to use the case law to force morality, to make it into statutory law, and to treat it as virtually on a par and of the same type as the apodictic law.[1]

The prophetic proclamation is noteworthy for its almost complete lack of interest in case law. The prophets were concerned with God's absolute demand as expressed in the apodictic 'Thou shalt'. They were impatient with the legal mentality which lived and moved and had its being within legal systems and were concerned chiefly with what could be legally enforced. In the Book of Jeremiah, for example, God's law is his way (5.4–5; cf. 6.15); it is his words (6.19; cf. Isa. 1.10), not only those spoken to Moses, but also his living word transmitted by the prophets (cf. 25.3–7; 26.4–5). On the other hand, the professional handlers of the law do not know God; they have followed things which do not profit (2.8): 'How can you say, We are wise, and the law of the Lord is with us? For, behold, into a lie the false pen of the scribes has made it' (8.8). The preoccupation with case law, with what can be enforced, was evidently to the prophets a stultifying procedure which enabled the lawyer to forget that the primary content of the covenant was the inward, personal requirement, 'Obey my voice, and I will be your

[1] These are the views defended in a paper by Professor George E. Mendenhall which is briefly summarized in the *Journal of Biblical Literature*, Vol. LXXI, 1952, p. vi.

God, and you shall be my people' (Jer. 7.23, 11.6–7; cf. 31.31ff.).

Jesus' teachings as collected in the Sermon on the Mount (Matt. 5–7) show the same exclusive concern with the apodictic, so that it was said: he taught 'as one who had authority, and not as their scribes' (Matt. 7.29). Behind these teachings is the continued insistence upon God's compelling will, obedience to which can spring only from inward and individual attachment which seeks first God's kingdom and his righteousness, which looks for 'perfection' like that of the heavenly Father (Matt. 5.48; 6.33). The legalists have betrayed the weightier matters of the law by their exclusive endeavour to bind all life within a case law used as an apodictic (Matt. 23). Hence the suspicion and fear of Jesus lay not so much in his exposition of apodictic law as in his denial of ultimate validity to case law, when the latter was used, not as a guide to life, but as a power to coerce life.

Such a viewpoint as expounded both by the prophets and Jesus implies that the individual members of the community possess a freedom for responsible decision amidst the details of daily life, because they must seek first and continually to express the righteousness of God. It is this freedom which the Apostle Paul expounded explicitly within the context of his doctrine of justification by faith. In the Pauline letters the Apostle has considerable advice to give to specific problems, but his methodology is not that of case law. He continually reflects the spirit of the apodictic law, and in seeking to apply it is quite conscious of the distinction between his opinion and God's word. For this reason his method is very different from the legal practice of Judaism wherein the application of apodictic law took the form of enforced case law. The New Testament never goes that far. Instead, it reasserts the absolute and compelling will of God for the community and at the same time the free, responsible decision which each individual must daily make if he has died with Christ and risen with him to new life. Even where we see the beginnings of a kind of canon law and of casuistry, the character of the New Testament's requirements as a 'law of freedom' is not lost.

2. In the second place, the ethics of the elect community is rooted in a Divine righteousness that has created a Kingdom of God, which though known now in Christ is yet to be completed by God. The community life of the Church of the New Testament thus reflects a two-sided situation. On the one hand, it exhibits the ethics of the Kingdom yet to be universally consummated; on the other hand, the ethics of a small, non-political group which understood itself as living in the interval before the consummation. It is thus difficult to think of the ethics of Jesus solely as an 'interim ethic', valid only for the interval (Albert Schweitzer), or solely as a 'kingdom ethic', as the description of the manner of the community in the age to come. Both are bound up in one another, neither can be denied; and they cannot be separated from one another without serious loss of meaning. C. H. Dodd has attempted to mediate between the two extreme positions taken concerning the 'interim ethic' and the 'kingdom ethic' by suggesting a view called 'realized eschatology'. The highly spiritualized outlook of the Gospel of John lends itself readily to this treatment, though the synoptic Gospels and the Epistles furnish more difficulty. According to Dodd, Jesus believed the eschatological process, the inbreaking of the Kingdom, had actually begun and was going on. The eschaton was at hand, and Christ was the way into it. The various passages which possess verbs in the future tense, indicating a future coming of the Kingdom, he believes to be accommodating modes of expression for the eternal breaking into the temporal. The

central point is that the new age, foretold by the prophets, had actually dawned in Christ.[1] This view is certainly correct in so far as it emphasizes the importance of the eschatological expectation in the New Testament and the belief that the eschatological process had actually begun. It is more difficult to follow when it seems to minimize the future consummation, not yet realized, which gives to the New Testament ethic its intensity and urgency.

The same atmosphere prevails among the prophets of the Old Testament, to whom the various historical crises, and particularly the Exile and Restoration, were the beginning of God's consummation and fulfilment of his purposes in history. The covenant law, on the other hand, did not possess this eschatological dimension. In it there was an ideal element, a sense of the revealed order of true community life in the elect society. While the specific laws of the covenant were an accommodation to the needs of that particular society, there was a continued attempt to get behind the laws to the real intent of God in them, so that the ordering of the covenant society was considered as a gracious act of God which at the beginning of the nations' history set the norm for community life. This conception of the ideal or revealed order is especially apparent in the institutions of the sabbatical and jubilee years, which, though ordained by the law, were evidently felt to be too impractical ever to be put into regular practice. This revealed order furnished the standard by which the actual order of society was judged, and the purposes of God observed within it furnished a clue to the prophets which enabled them to portray the eschatological meaning of contemporary events and the future intention of God. The New Testament is the direct continuation and partial fulfilment of the

[1] Cf. C. H. Dodd, *The Parables of the Kingdom*, London, 1935, pp. 107–9.

prophetic eschatological expectation, and it ends with the hope and certainty of the complete consummation of the new society at the second advent.

The eschatological rootage of New Testament ethics is thus fixed in the knowledge of God's working in history and in the certainty that history has its fulfilment in God's Kingdom. There is, therefore, no faith that ethics or an ethical system will of itself inaugurate or hasten the arrival of the Kingdom. Judaism and the liberal idealism of the western world have had this much in common: both have believed that obedience to the law, or moral integrity, could of itself be effectual in hastening the millennium. Yet the life of the community of the New Testament did not have this purpose. God was inaugurating his own Kingdom by his own methods, using to be sure, the witness of the elect; but the ethics of the community had not the purpose of 'building the kingdom'. It was rather considered as the obedient and normal life of a community that was 'in Christ'. It was simply 'following Christ'; it was a discipleship which God would reward in his own way but it was not considered as a necessary step without which the new age would not arrive. Since God requires it, it is essential; but its precise efficacy in relation to the Kingdom is his alone to decide.

In the Old Testament the viewpoint toward the efficacy of ethics is similar. In the covenant theology obedience to the law of God was a pre-supposition of the revealed order. Consequently, proper community life under God would be accompanied by the complete blessing of God with the resultant peace, security, 'perfection' and prosperity which God desired to confer upon his people (cf. Lev. 26 and Deut. 28). Obedience and blessing were tied together in one ideal order which in itself was envisaged as God's kingdom. Such an order, however, never came into being. As revelation, however, it furnished the historians and prophets with the clue to the interpretation of history and to the intention of God to create in history that which he had revealed. In the prophetic proclamation, however, obedience is efficacious only in averting the Divine judgment upon the elect. Community ethics affect the nature of God's immediate acts toward his chosen people, but their purpose is not the 'building' of God's universal Kingdom. God is not considered to be dependent upon our goodness, but is at work in his own way, with his own purposes which cannot be defeated. A proper community life is one which issues from grateful response to God's loving acts. It is God's will, the keeping of which is its own reward. It is the people's calling or election which is to be followed in love, though also in fear and trembling, for God is righteous.

It would appear, then, that the perspective in which the community life of the elect must be viewed in the Bible as a whole is to be discovered in the conception of Kingdom. The nature of life within the Kingdom is known in two different ways: in the *revealed* order of the covenant community, to which the *actual* situation in the covenant society is compared, and in the new order in the New Covenant, which, promised by God through the prophets, actually came into being in Christ. Since the first reveals the intention of God of which the latter is the fulfilment, one might think that the two should be the same. Their relation is complicated, however, by the fact that the first is an accommodation to the needs of a people who were a political and national organism, faced with the problems of justice, security and well-being in one country at one particular time. Consequently, the covenant law of Israel is not a static system of propositions of universal validity. Its first and primary relevance is for the life of Israel in the pre-Christian age. It is the revelation of

God in one historical epoch.[1] New Testament ethics, on the other hand, reflect the different situation of the elect community. The early Christian community was not a political organism with responsibility for the justice and security of a nation. This responsibility was in the hands of a pagan government, to which Christians were subject. The Apostle Paul believed that since the moral purpose of the law of the state was good, Christians were not free to disregard it or to use their liberty in Christ in any way contrary to it. Government is a terror, not to good conduct, but to bad. It is an institution of God for this purpose, and taxes must be paid to it for conscience's sake. Neighbourly love fulfils all law and does no wrong (Rom. 13). On the other hand, after the Church had received persecution, its attitude toward the Roman government was evidently altered (e.g. Rev.). New Testament ethics are thus accommodated to the situation of a nonpolitical community which is not a nation among nations. Consequently, we have no knowledge of what the Apostle Paul might have taught had he been in the place of the prophets of Israel. Yet the life of both communities may perhaps be held together if we recall that both are the product of, and responsive to, the righteousness of God. In both community life was the product of an obedient love. The first was concerned with a revealed order for the life of a nation; the second

[1] The use of Old Testament law in a static manner by the modern Church, for example to justify the segregation *within* the *ecclesia* as well as in civil society, is thus automatically suspect. The intent of the law was to provide full communion even for the sojourner. Nevertheless, certain exceptions were made, as Deut. 23.2–6; 25.17–19 appear to indicate. These exceptions cannot be taken as normative for similar exceptions in the modern Church because they are clearly in violation of the law's deeper intention. They must be understood, therefore, as products of historical conditioning which in Christ are done away.

was the alteration and fulfilment of that order in the light of Christ and in a radically different social and political situation. To confess Christ as Lord of the Church and Lord of the Scripture is to confess him also as the righteousness of God. If the Scripture finds its unity in him, then community life under both the Old and the New Covenants, in so far as it is a response to the righteousness of God in different political situations, must be a relevant concern of the Church.

E. The New Society in the New Age

Biblical faith, knowing as it did the true nature of community and of the individual within it, nevertheless also knew the present corrupted state, even of the elect. Yet the knowledge of the grace of God and of his purpose in history did not permit despair and disillusion. The eschatological faith bore men up in the knowledge that what now is will not so remain. We must now ask, therefore, how the future is to resolve the problem of individual and community.

Our object here is not to canvass all the biblical teachings with regard to the life in the consummation of the People of God, but to select those features which bear especially upon the question of man in society. The study of the goal of the redeemed society in terms of its transcendent, trans-historical character might at first seem to be remote from a concern with this question. On the contrary, the biblical view of man, and of man in community, is only rightly grasped when the eschatological aspect of the question is taken into account. Whether we consider the matter with respect to the resurrection of the individual or with respect to the social and corporate aspects of the consummation, implications are immediately at hand for our basic problem.

We call attention to one aspect of method at the outset.

While we are not first of all occupied with the question of the Church in the present age, yet we cannot altogether neglect matters related to it. For in the New Testament features of the consummation are seen as already present in the life of the people of God in the present age. This is only one aspect of the close inter-relation of the topics into which our general project is subdivided.

1. The significance of our theme and of the evidence which we shall adduce will be clearer if we first call to mind as foils certain aspects of pagan or secular views of eschatology and destiny.

(a) Even apart from belief in the survival of the individual a recognition of his social significance in this life may appear, as the literature of Israel attests. Before the rise of the belief in resurrection the faithful Israelite recognized that the meaning of his personal existence was bound up with the life of his people and with the covenant on which it was based. The future of the people and the promises made to them were in a sense his, though he would not share in them during his own life. In the modern world an analogous but secular view often obtains, according to which the individual has an 'immortality in the race'. But in such cases the covenant responsibilities of the devout Israelite and his covenant safeguards as a person are by no means always implied. This secular doctrine of man is quite compatible with master race or totalitarian conceptions.

(b) More sophisticated conceptions of the immortality of man are based on the idea of his share through reason in that which abides unchanged. Through our participation in that which is timeless we are ourselves exempt from corruption and death. Yet such a view fails to affirm the personal life in its social relations.

'If we then press the question, what becomes of this "I" when death destroys the body which has been its seat and organ, its immortality is conceived as some kind of absorption into universal Mind, involving the elimination of everything which constitutes individuality. For individuality is bound up with the particular, the contingent, the accidental. Thus such a view of immortality fails to affirm the permanence of individual personality. . . . The idea that the individual is absorbed in the Absolute as a drop of water in the ocean is congenial to some mystical types of religion, but it is alien to Christianity in its classical forms, for which the infinite worth of the individual soul is a postulate.'[1]

The difficulty with all such views, whether in ancient gnosticism or in modern rationalism or mysticism, is that they presuppose a psychology which separates reason or spirit from body, and the individual from the historical life of his fellows.

(c) There is finally the view common in all ages, one which penetrates widely into Christianity, which rests upon the idea of the 'immortality of the soul'. Here the 'soul' is viewed as sharply distinguishable from the body, as a 'simple' subject, indissoluble, and therefore able to survive the dissolution of the body.

'This conception of the soul is highly abstract. To carry over into another plane of being a bare consciousness of personal identity can hardly be compared with that hope of everlasting life to which the religious consciousness aspires. . . . In actual fact, human personality, as we know

[1] C. H. Dodd, 'The Communion of Saints', The Ingersoll Lecture on the Immortality of Man, *The Harvard Divinity School Annual*, 1935-6, p. 8.

it in ourselves, is not "simple" but infinitely complex. In particular it is constituted out of personal relations.'[1]

As Professor Dodd implies, such a view of man, even though it admits some kind of belief in survival, does not envisage him in thoroughly responsible social relations. All of the examples we have adduced indicate, by contrast, the imperative significance for a right understanding of man-in-community of (1) the biblical view of man and (2) the biblical view of the resurrection and the communion of saints.

2. The Bible itself makes clear the connection of its view of man in the consummation with its view of man as creature. No greater mistake can be made than to look upon the New Testament teaching regarding the resurrection and the life to come as gratuitous features which can be set aside. To view these elements as an 'otherworldly' and foreign intrusion in the Bible, introduced through the play of fantasy or with a compensatory motive, conscious or unconscious, is to overlook the teleology and promise which run through the Bible. It is also to fail to recognize that the doctrine of the end is connected with its doctrine of the beginning. Man delivered from the Fall and its effects enters finally into a condition which is *at least* a restoration of that relation to God and his fellows for which he was created.

The Bible's view of time and history establishes an intimate continuity between the successive phases of the world-drama, so that the end-state is a true outcome and fulfilment of what has gone before. This appears, indeed, in the theme of judgment and in the assignment of rewards and penalties. It appears more significantly in the use of metaphors and symbols which imply the fulfilment in the age to come of gains, experiences, labours in this age. Figures of growth, building

[1] *Ibid.*, pp. 7–8.

and reaping are used with reference to gains carried over into the new age. God's work in man in the redeemed society, both in the individual and in the community, always liable to frustrations in this age, has its sure fruitage in the age to come. The overall continuity is indicated by the fact that the end is to be as God intended it.

W. A. Beardslee has made a study of Paul's use of the term *ergon*, work, and its cognates and related terms which is significant here.[1] Though Paul sees the activity of unregenerate man as 'unfruitful', and though he sees even the labours of apostles and believers as at the mercy of destructive adversaries in this age, yet the work of the Christian always bears fruit without fail in the consummation. What Paul has in mind here above all is the building up of the Church, the growth to maturity of the individual believer, and the furthering of the Divine love (*agape*) and spiritual blessings of the community, the Body of Christ.

The doctrine of the resurrection *of the body* confirms this insistence on the continuity between the personal life of this age and the person-in-community life of the age to come. Likewise with the conceptions of corporate or world eschatology. The transcendental representations of the world to come are genetically related to earlier Jewish Messianic conceptions anticipating a strictly mundane felicity. Such symbols as those of the feast, the kingdom, the heavenly city, or the Rest, indicate transparently the continuity of the social goals of the new age with this-worldly community life and ideals. This is not merely because men must use images of the visible world to describe the world invisible. It is rather because the goal is seen in relation to the course run, and the new creation in relation to the old.

The relation of the new age to the old is best symbolized by

[1] This study is thus far unpublished.

the figure of travail and childbirth (Isa. 26.17–18; 66.7–9; cf. 45.10; Micah 4.9–10; 5.3; also Mark 13.8; Rev. 12.2); also by the related figures of harvest, gathering and reaping (Rev. 14.15; John 4.36; Gal. 6.8), or of blossoming or the leafing out of spring or summer (Isa. 35.1–2; 61.11; cf. 45.8; also Mark 13.28ff.). The Bible also offers the figure of an object reshaped, i.e. the potter's work (Jer. 18.1–6; Rom. 9.23–24); or an object or scene glorified (Is. 60.1ff., 19–20); or of that which is washed or cleansed (Isa. 4.2–4; Jer. 33.8); or of a city transformed (Isa. 54.11–12; Rev. 21, 22); or the dead quickened (Ezek. 37.1–14; Isa. 53.9; Hosea 13.14); or a person or group inspired (Isa. 42.1; 59.21; Joel 2.28–29; Acts 2, etc.). In all such figures the continuities are implied along with the novelty, but some suggest more clearly the idea of teleological fulfilment, particularly those of childbirth and harvest.

The biblical conception of nature is closely linked with its view of man and has a bearing on the theme of the present section. In Old Testament thought man is not divorced from nature, nor on the other hand is he identified with nature. This has important implications for man's ultimate destiny. Just as individual *and* society are linked by a significant nexus which continues in the new age, so man-in-society *and* nature are linked by a significant nexus which also continues in the new age. The importance of this relatedness of man and nature appears when we contrast it with views which either subject man to matter and its laws, or which propose a dualism according to which man's peculiar being and destiny are divorced from nature, with all the corollaries of asceticism and false spirituality which ensue.

According to the Bible man is made of the dust of the earth and is closely related to the animal creation. His relatedness to nature is viewed as so intimate that what affects the one affects the other, and nature shares in the effects of man's first sin. The New Testament makes it clear that nature and the cosmic powers share in the events of redemption, and it is anticipated that man in the consummation will continue in relation to a redeemed nature. The transformations of nature in the end-time are suggested in various ways in the prophets, in Rom. 8, and in Revelation. Transcendent pictures of the Promised Land, the New Jerusalem, the defeat of the discordant cosmic powers, the new heaven and the new earth all bear testimony to the fact that the conception of human fulfilment assumes in some sense a renewed creation as the necessary theatre of the blessed existence of the communion of saints. Here the 'sacramental' significance of nature is validated in the same way that the 'sacramental' significance of the body or flesh is validated by the conception of the resurrection of the body. Indeed, the two ideas are inseparably related since a 'body' involves a realm of nature. Where eudemonistic conceptions appear in connection with the New Jerusalem or age-to-come we have only an inevitable expression of the Bible's consistent view that the creation is good.

The Bible's doctrine of man in the life of the world to come only unfolds, therefore, motifs which are present in its general doctrine of man. The worth of the individual is not asserted principally upon the ground that he has an 'eternal soul' or that he is an 'immortal being' but rather on the more general ground that he is made in God's image. The responsibility of the community to the individual and his claims to a degree of freedom of action are not to be asserted principally upon the basis of eschatological sanctions, though these are relevant, even those drawn from the doctrine of rewards and penalties. But they should be asserted rather upon the basis of the more general doctrine of the intra-personal and covenant character of the people of God. Here the eschatological conceptions of the Kingdom of God and the New Jerusalem serve only to confirm the essential insights of faith with regard to man in this age.

3. Fundamental to the very idea of survival as well as to the social concept of the new age is the doctrine of man in Israel, particularly its understanding of the *self*. In contrast to the views noted in section 1 above, the self or identity is not associated with some particular faculty or organ of the human being, whether his psyche, his spirit or his reason. The self is the total creature. Man is thought of as a willing, acting being. If one term rather than another suggests his personal identity, it is the term 'heart', but the 'heart' is not a part or a faculty of the man. And the mutual relations of the individual with family, tribe and people are a part of the constitution of the self. We have here not merely an evidence of primitive tribal views of solidarity, but a psychology which modern study has validated in important respects. 'No man is an island.' The individual lives in a web of relations that reach out to other men, and that reach back to those before him and forward to those that live after him. And these relations constitute in a real sense a considerable part of his identity and of his immortality. It would follow that any conception of genuine survival of death would necessarily link the individual with his social context, since his very identity is not defined apart from it. It would also follow that survival would be integral in character; that is, perpetuation of the willing, acting self in some embodied sense (and so capable of participation)—though this corollary was tardy in establishing itself.

As Jewish eschatology changed under the impact of new circumstances, we see the rise of a demand for a share in the new age for the righteous dead, at first only for the patriarchs and martyrs, and then for the righteous generally. The naïve idea of physical reanimation is employed at first to assign them a share in the time of fulfilment. This conception asserts in any case its concretely social character. The trend to a transcendental conception of the new age represents a spiritualizing of the eschatology which, despite occasional reversions, preserves the main insights. Hellenistic Judaism tended to an individualistic view of immortality but the main stream of thought safeguarded the social emphasis.

4. Without undertaking an exposition of the events of the end-time as variously portrayed, attention should be called to their significance. The variety of dramatic representations of the judgment reflect a variety of situations. The Day of Yahweh of the earlier period, the work of the anointed scion of David, the coming to judgment of God himself, or of the Son of Man, or the *parousia* of Jesus, each carry with them particular subordinate detail. The import of all these variant expectations is the separation of the true people of God from the wicked, and the inauguration of the time of salvation, together with the removal of sin and evil from the creation.

What is of particular significance is the transformation of the idea of judgment in some writings of the New Testament. The process of final judgment begins with the work of Christ in his life, death and resurrection (and indeed in the Fourth Gospel is largely *identified* with this work), continues in the interim between his Resurrection and his Second Coming, and is completed at his return. Judgment here is eschatological (cf. the revelation of the wrath of God in Rom. 10). Just as salvation is proleptic in the New Testament, so is judgment. The consummation of the Redeemed Society is already in course, before the *parousia* or Second Coming, *pari passu* with the elimination of evil by judgment; but the very process of judgment becomes a foil for the call to repentance.

It is against this background that Paul sees the world-wide

mission of the apostles and the Church. Here the never-resolved question of universalism emerges. The judgment implies final reprobation of some, yet it is also set forth as an occasion of repentance. Moreover, universal salvation is implied in certain passages of the New Testament, whether in Rom. 11, or in the contrast of the two Adams in Romans and elsewhere, or in the intercession of Christ for all men viewed as necessarily effective. What is especially significant for the theme of society and the individual are the criteria of judgment. The ethical tests implied, reflect the character of the Redeemed Community. But God's dealing with those judged will inevitably be consistent with his gracious character and with the loving purpose which is the final determinant of the consummation.

5. Jesus and the first Christians acclaim in various ways the imminence and indeed the presence of the new age. The New Testament views of the Kingdom, of the New Jerusalem, and of the redeemed society of the end-time are both futuristic and 'realized'.

(a) We note first the future aspect. Here the goal is placed beyond the awaited *parousia* and last judgment. Our classic portrayals of it are found in the Apocalypse, though it is represented also in many passages in the Synoptic Gospels which speak of the messianic banquet, of the new people to which the vineyard will be entrusted, and of the 'gathering' of the elect at the coming of the Son of Man. It is also referred to in those passages in Paul's letters in which the older schema of the Second Coming is presupposed, as in the Thessalonian Epistles and in I Corinthians. In this aspect the goal of the Redeemed Society takes over the anticipations of the Old Testament with respect to the social character of the Kingdom, the agency of God in its establishment—now through Christ—the transcendence of ethnic lines, and the banishment of evil whether natural or moral. We note also that in some respects the end is as the beginning, Omega as Alpha, the original unity and felicity of man in creation is restored, and the description of Paradise in Genesis repeats itself in the Revelation. We have already noted that the creation itself is renewed in conjunction with the renewal of the race.

In what concerns the social organization of the Redeemed Community in the consummation, varying patterns can be adduced from the Bible. Basic is the idea that God is king and the people are his servants. Theocratic political forms changed in the life of Israel in different periods and reflected themselves in conceptions of the future. In the New Testament we find the corresponding basic view that Christ is Lord and the believers his servants, yet all under God. In the church there are vocations and services, but secular conceptions of rank are excluded. On the other hand, modern secular ideas of individualism and egalitarianism are excluded by the doctrine of the Spirit and the emphasis on diversity of social function in the one Body. The members of the one Body owe their various qualifications and roles to the One Spirit and the common Lord. Since we are here specially concerned with the consummation it is enough to say that the conception of the Redeemed Society in the New Age articulates itself in accord with the figures of the 'Body' or the 'Vine' as suggested below. The special role of the apostles and martyrs in the portrayals of the New Age in the Apocalypse and in Matthew, is, however, an example of the tendency toward hierarchical views which the Church found not incompatible with Jesus' warning against Gentile views of rank and precedence.

(b) The full significance of the New Age appears only when we give attention to those New Testament portrayals which effectively depart from the Jewish framework of *parousia* and judgment. Here we have to do especially with elements in the teaching of Jesus and of Paul, with the Epistle to the Hebrews, with the Epistle to the Ephesians, and with the Fourth Gospel. Here in one form or another the eschatological community is already clearly in existence. The believers have already passed out of death into life, or have had access already to the heavenly Tabernacle, and the judgment day falls into comparative insignificance. The Church as the Body of Christ (Paul), or the new and perfect humanity (Ephesians), or the new temple (*passim*), or as 'Mt. Zion ... the city of the living God, the heavenly Jerusalem ... the general assembly and church of the firstborn' (Hebrews), or the 'one flock' and 'vine' (John), is already living the life eternal of God and of the glorified Christ. Its members are already dead and risen. Indeed these who lived by faith in the past are themselves sharers now in that 'city that hath foundations whose builder and maker is God'. Those 'just men' are 'now made perfect', i.e. are risen into its fellowship, who apart from us could not be so made perfect (Heb. 11.39-40).[1]

This New Testament conception of the consummation as realized in the present age and passing without interruptions into the limitless glory of God has one of its best characterizations in the Letter to the Ephesians:

'the household of God, built upon the foundations of the apostles and prophets, Christ Jesus himself being the chief cornerstone, in whom the whole structure is joined together and grows into a holy temple in the Lord; in whom you also are built into it for a dwelling place of God in the Spirit' (2.19-22).

'speaking the truth in love, we are to grow up in every way into him who is the head, into Christ, from whom the

[1] See Dodd, op. cit., p. 13.

whole body, joined and knit together by every joint with which it is supplied, when each part is working properly, makes bodily growth and upbuilds itself in love' (4.15–16).

These passages clarify the passage which speaks of the 'full grown humanity' in close connection with the body of Christ and the fulness (*pleroma*) of Christ (4.12–13).

The evidence before us shows that the goal of the Redeemed Society presents us not only with a social or corporate idea of the consummation, but also with one in which all earthly distinctions are transcended. Its life and continuance beyond death rests on the power and Spirit of God, and its mutual love is the manifestation in the communion of saints of the love of God.

IV

THE PEOPLE OF GOD
IN THE WORLD

HAVING attempted in Chapter II to describe the biblical
conception of man and society in the world, and in Chapter
III the new society as the people of God, we must now turn
our attention to the relationship between the two. It has been
shown that the Bible forthrightly sets forth man's social
nature, so that there is no understanding of true personality
apart from a people. Accordingly, all sin has social consequences and is both individual and social, voluntarist and
constituent, at the same time. Salvation is also conceived in
both individual and corporate terms, so that the biblical
conception of the Kingdom of God which fulfils present and
past history is not portrayed as an amorphous mass society but
instead as the true community. It fulfils the revealed order of
the new people already established, in which man the individual as a responsible person derives meaning from the fact
that he has been placed by God as labourer within the responsible society. The new community created by God is in
a real sense the 'first-fruits' of the eschatological community
(e.g. James 1.18; Rev. 14.4). At the present time, however, it
exists in a pagan world which is constantly invading it. It is in
continual danger of betrayal, but at the same time it has been
given a vocation in the world of such a nature that it must
come to terms constantly with pagan man and society.

A. RESPONSIBILITY FOR THE WORLD

The first thing we may say about the relationship between the people of God and the peoples of the world, therefore, is that the former is burdened with a God-given responsibility before and for the latter. A summary of one aspect of their responsibility has been seen by the Church to be contained in Jesus' 'Great Commission' to his disciples (Matt. 28.18–20). The first task of the Church in the world is that of the proclamation of the Gospel which has been given it, and this involves teaching, baptism into the new community of Christ and obedience ('to observe all things whatsoever I have commanded you'). It is clear that the Bible understands no means of salvation for man and his societies in the world except through conversion, and the People of God are an agent whereby this will be accomplished.

The testimony by word is, of course, only one means of witness bearing. Suffering is to be borne as an integral part of discipleship, for the martyr witnesses, as did Jesus, with his life. The redemptive nature of suffering and its firm place in the individual's calling are deeply embedded in the New Testament's conception of responsibility in the world; and for this reason the figure of the Suffering Servant of Second Isaiah played a much larger inspirational role in the early Church than evidently it did in the synagogue, because it was understood to interpret the life of Christ, and through Christ was in a sense applicable to the disciple.

Whereas the roles of missionary and martyr were confined to comparatively few, every member of the community was to exhibit *before* the world the fruits of his loyalty to Christ. Gospel and ethics were so bound up in one another that the individual understood an ethical urgency placed upon his innermost being; and that is true even in the most apocalyptic passages of New Testament expectation. For this reason, most of the ethical teachings of the New Testament have to do either with the inner life of the disciple or with his relations to the brotherhood. The Epistles abound with exhortations concerned with the fruits of the Spirit as they should be seen within the fellowship of Christ: e.g. 'love, joy, peace, patience, kindness, goodness, faithfulness, gentleness, self-control. . . . If we live by the Spirit, let us also walk by the Spirit. Let us have no self-conceit, no provoking of one another, no envy of one another. . . . Bear one another's burdens, and so fulfil the law of Christ' (Gal. 5.16ff., R.S.V.; cf. I Cor. 13–14; Jas.; I Pet., etc.).

Essentially the same ethic of brotherly love within the community is also enjoined upon the individual in his relations with those not of the 'household of faith'. C. J. Cadoux maintains that this is clearest in the teaching of Jesus, particularly in the widest possible meaning given to the identity of one's neighbour (e.g. Matt. 5.43–48 and especially the words: 'if you salute your brethren only, what do ye more than others?' During the course of the first century, however, there was an increasing sense of the isolation of Church from the world with the result that there was 'a growing tendency to narrow the circle, so that Christian love becomes love for the brotherhood'.[1] When, for example, I Pet. 2.17 says: 'Honour all men. Love the brotherhood. Fear God. Honour the king', love appears confined. Indeed, the thought of the Epistle shows little concern for the Divine love directed to non-Christians. And this may have furnished the basis, however slight, for the charge of 'hatred against

[1] *The Early Church and the World*, (Edinburgh, 1925), pp. 91, 159. This increasing isolation was not mere clannishness, but the result of persecution.

mankind' which was levelled against Christians in the persecution of Nero.[1]

Nevertheless, the same epistle says that one should 'be ready always to give an answer to every man that asketh you a reason of the hope that is in you, *but with meekness and respect*' (I Pet. 3.15). Even the simplest believer bore a responsibility before pagans, for Christians should shine among them 'as lights in the world' (Phil. 2.15). The nature of conduct before and toward outsiders was of great importance. All actions and attitudes considered wrong by both pagans and Christians must be avoided. Great care must be exercised in securing and keeping a good reputation: 'to live quietly, to mind you own affairs, and to work with your hands . . . so that you may command the respect of outsiders' (I Thess. 4.11–12, R.S.V.; cf. also I Cor. 14.23–25). 'We aim at what is honourable not only in the Lord's sight but also in the sight of men' (II Cor. 8.21; cf. Rom. 12.17; Col. 4.5). Indeed, noble living is a means of overcoming evil and shaming slanderers ('that they may see your good deeds and glorify God . . .' 'it is God's will that by doing right you should put to silence the ignorance of foolish men', I Pet. 2.12, 15; R.S.V.). In all conduct before and toward the world the Christian is responsible to do good to all, to avoid envy and vengeance, to submit to wrongdoing: 'if your enemy is hungry, feed him; if he is thirsty, give him drink; for by so doing you will heap burning coals upon his head. Do not be overcome by evil, but overcome evil with good' (Rom. 12.20-21, R.S.V.; cf. I Thess. 5.15).

This application of the ethic of love to non-Christian individuals may perhaps indicate a significant shift in attitude in at least one particular from that in the Old Testament. There appears to be no thought whatever that it is the proper

[1] Tacitus, *Annals*, Book 15.44.

duty of Christians to be the instrument of the Lord's wrath upon pagan society. In the Old Testament, however, such a view was the explanation in part of the meaning of the Conquest of Canaan. Israel was the agent of the Divine judgment upon evil societies (e.g. Deut. 9.4–5). In a number of the eschatological passages in the prophets one infers that the new Israel will be one instrument among others in humbling the pride of the wicked (e.g. Ezek. 38–39, though always within the context of the righteousness of God). This view was especially prominent in the theology devised for the Davidic dynasty in Jerusalem concerning the role which the Anointed of David would play in the eschatological wars (e.g. Pss. 2; 18; 20; 72; 110). Such a conclusion, one must admit, is largely inferential because the emphasis is entirely upon God's activity and not upon the temporal means whereby that activity is manifest. And human agency is only one means; great emphasis is placed poetically upon the use of natural scourges and convulsions (e.g. Ezek. 38.22; Zech. 14.6–19). In the apocalyptic passages of the New Testament the tendency to be observed in Jewish apocalyptic is continued: namely, to emphasize almost exclusively the divine warfare with little said about the means of its accomplishment. From the fact that the Church did not consider itself called to be an active instrument of judgment one might indeed conclude that the ethical inferences drawn from the life and death of Jesus did not permit any such view of the community's calling. Yet one must also recall the situation of this community. It was a non-political society, small in number, with no public responsibility. Its members as yet held no public office which required them to take responsible coercive action. It was a society within a state, whereas Israel was a nation whose actions over against other nations demanded interpretation. That God could use this nation as a coercive instrument was thus affirmed, while it was also seen that other nations were instruments of judgment upon it. To interpret history in a biblical manner requires such a view, even though later interpreters may challenge this or that interpretation given in specific instances.

In the New Testament, then, it is clear that we have much more material dealing with the responsibility of the community of Christ to its Lord *before* the world than we have of an active responsibility for the salvation of the world. The reason is that salvation is in the hands of God, and in Christ God offers it to the world. To this fact the Church is to bear witness, while it lives loyal to the inner covenant. No more than this is expected of the new community, because the conversion of the nations from their present societies to the kingdom of God involves a great cosmic struggle against rebellious powers which only God can successfully conduct. The whole emphasis thus lies, not upon the community's task and ability to win the world to Christ, but upon the active work of the living God who accomplishes what man cannot, and who is and will be undefeated.[1]

It is in this context that we are to understand the Old Testament. Otherwise its resources for the question of responsibility would be unquestionably and understandably meagre. Central to the thought of the Old Testament is God's claim to sovereignty over the whole world. This meant to Israel that the treasure God had given her by Act and Word was of infinite worth and would be shared by all men because that is what God had decreed and because that is the ultimate purpose for which it was given. Foreigners shall hear of it, and

[1] A qualifying statement should be added, however. The New Testament Epistles were written to the churches and were concerned largely with internal matters. In Acts, where the Church is witnessing, a somewhat different emphasis is to be observed.

when they come to Jerusalem their prayers will be heard
(I Kings 8.41ff.); the temple is to be a house of prayer for all
peoples (Isa. 56.6–7); from it the Word of the Lord will go
out to the nations, for Jerusalem will be the capital of the
world (Isa. 2.2ff.; Micah 4.1ff.). When that happens the world
will have peace for only then will all acknowledge God as
Lord and Judge. Indeed 'the full fruits of Israel's faith can only
be hers when all men share that faith, and therefore share its
fruits'.[1] God's blessing to his community is inextricably tied
to his struggle for universal dominion; he has decreed this to
be so in his heavenly council.[2] Meanwhile, as a response to
what God has done, believers can be so moved with gratitude
that they are impelled to sing forth his praise to all peoples.
A number of passages in the Psalms could be cited as indication
of this mood, of which the following is typical: 'I will give
thanks to thee, O Lord, among the peoples; I will sing praises
to thee among the nations. For thy steadfast love is great to
the heavens, thy faithfulness to the clouds' (Ps. 57.9–10;
R.S.V.).

Yet the *dominant* emphasis of the Old Testament is not
concerned with Israel's active work among the nations, but
instead with God's work, with the fulfilling of his purpose,

[1] H. H. Rowley, *The Missionary Message of the Old Testament*,
London, 1944, pp. 40–41.

[2] E.g. such a passage as Ps. 67: 'May God be gracious unto us and
bless us . . . that thy way may be known upon the earth, thy salvation
among all nations. . . . God shall bless us, and all the ends of the earth
shall reverence him' (or 'May God bless us, and may all the ends of the
earth reverence him'). Similarly, in Genesis God's blessing of the
Patriarchs is to the end that by Israel all the families of the earth shall
bless themselves (Gen. 12.3; 18.18; 28.14; 22.18; 26.4): that is, there
is a definite relation between the blessing of the Chosen and the
blessing of the world, not because the evidence was then seen, but
because it has been decreed by God and God will work it out.

for which Israel is his passive instrument. By his gracious and mighty acts in and for Israel, he will make himself known to the peoples, whereas Israel's active responsibility is a profound loyalty, devotion and obedience to him alone. And in this sense the major role of the called community is precisely similar to that in the New Testament. In prophetic eschatology and in the conquest of Canaan, however, we have noted above the active role Israel played and was conceived yet to play as the agent of Divine judgment. On the other hand, in two books, as is well known, the redemptive mission of Israel is clearly affirmed, and in doing so, the Old Testament is generally acknowledged to have penetrated most deeply into the intention of God for his community in the world.

(1) The setting of the Book of Jonah is placed by the Post-Exilic author in the Assyrian period. In this book there is little interest in the prophetic message of the prophet; instead the concern is with what he was and thought. He did not wish to be God's agent of mercy to the pagan world, and the thought of God's merciful concern for his people's enemy angered him. By implication the author is condemning Israel's misinterpretation of the doctrine of her election and is affirming her prophetic responsibility even to her enemy, to the end that repentance may take place and forgiveness be secured.

(2) In Second Isaiah (Isa. 40–55) the figure of the Servant of the Lord is a fluid conception which, in a manner typically biblical, holds within itself both community and individual. As in the New Testament where Christ can be presented both as the Body and as the Head of the Body, so the Servant is Israel and also the representative who in himself embodies Israel. He is the whole Israel called to be a missionary community; he is the individual member of that community called to embody that mission; he is also the one who will carry the mission far beyond anything hitherto reached. At a

131

time when political Israel was destroyed and scattered, he was called to bring forth justice to the nations, yet not by might but by weakness ('a bruised reed shall he not break', Isa. 42.1–4). The political power of the Messianic office has been placed by God on the Persian king, Cyrus (45.1–13), not on the Servant. The latter is not an active instrument of punishment; God has made him a saving 'covenant of the people, a light to the nations, to open the blind eyes and deliver the prisoner from the dungeon' (42.6–7; cf. 49.6). He knows 'how to sustain with a word him that is weary' (50.4, R.S.V.) though he has suffered scourging and shame from which he has not hid his face. As one terribly afflicted, he was passed by, unesteemed (53.2–3). Yet because of the manner in which his suffering has been accepted and borne, all men shall be led to confess: 'All we like sheep have gone astray; we have turned every one to his own way; and the Lord has laid on him the iniquity of us all' (53.6). God will vindicate his mission because he poured out his soul unto death, and was numbered with the rebellious; yet he bore the sin of many and for the rebellious he interceded' (53.12).

To be the mediator of the saving covenant, to open blind eyes and deliver the prisoner, to bring good tidings to the poor, to proclaim the year of the Lord's favour, the day of his salvation[1] (61.1–2), and to accept vicarious suffering while interceding for those whose sin is being borne—such is the Servant's mission in and to the world. In the description of it

[1] The Hebrew word usually rendered 'vengeance' in Isa. 61.2 does not mean a process of getting even for wrongs done oneself. It is solely a prerogative of God and refers to his vindication of himself in the earth. This vindication is the hoped for salvation to the community of the faith, though it is a time of just judgment for the wicked. For this reason, the translation of the word in a particular case depends upon which aspect of God's working is uppermost in a writer's mind. In Isa. 61 the context indicates that 'salvation' is meant.

one feels very near the New Testament. Indeed Second Isaiah was primary source material for the Early Church's understanding of Christ and of the mission of the new community.[1] Of particular significance for us here is the 'corporate personality' of the Servant. By its means the writer is enabled to describe not only the One who embodies the mission, but also the mission of the community so embodied and as well of the individual members of the community. We note too the redemptive and pacific role of the Servant; he is not an active or coercive agent of Divine justice any more than is the community of the New Testament. Yet here too we must recall the historical situation: a people without power in the world, a broken nation which is no longer a political entity. God himself still works coercively, however, and the pagan Cyrus is his instrument 'to subdue nations' and to 'break in pieces bronze doors' (Isa. 45.1–2).

It is quite clear, therefore, that the conception of responsibility *before* and *to* the world is indeed prominent in biblical thinking, but it is conceived in terms of responsibility to the active Lord of the world rather than in terms of ethical humanitarianism. God is directing and conducting the universal battle with evil, and the new community, struggling constantly with the meaning of its calling in the world, could conceive of its immediate task in different ways depending upon the situation in which it was placed at a particular time. Its first responsibility was always one of loyalty to its Lord which involved love of the brethren and indefatigable intolerance toward all forms of idolatry which would remove and destroy the cornerstone of the community's structure. In certain situations this primary loyalty appears to have exhausted the conception of responsibility in the world. Yet

[1] See especially H. H. Rowley, *The Servant of the Lord and Other Essays*, London 1952, Chaps. 1 and 2.

133

in other situations, and particularly in certain great spokesmen for the faith, a far more active role was held before the community, its precise nature varying according to the times and minds involved.

B. WITHDRAWAL FROM THE WORLD

Inasmuch as the Bible conceives the world as in alienation from God and subjected to sin, one might expect that the new society would find its life in complete separation and isolation from the world. Yet, as we have seen, the biblical attitude toward the world permitted no such comparatively simple solution.

1. There were indeed movements and tendencies toward withdrawal. One is to be seen in Jewish apocalypticism with its attitude of virtually complete pessimism toward the course of current life. History is projected into a straight, downward slanting line running from the beginning to the end. This line has no centre; it has beginning and end, but only *after* the end will the Messiah come. God has abandoned much of his active power over history to the fallen angels. Hence the life of the faithful has little meaning now, other than perseverance in suffering through hope in the future vindication. This attitude persisted in certain parts of the New Testament, especially in the time when the Church was suffering persecution. The 'little children' addressed in the Johannine Epistles, for example, are a group envisaged in almost complete isolation, having no more to do with the world than was absolutely necessary. They were of God, while the whole world was at its last hour, completely in the power of the Evil One (I John 2.18; 5.19). They were thus simply to wait patiently, living by the principle of love for one another, and concentrating their energies to exclude the world and its false deceivers who are the antichrist (e.g. II John 7–11). The

apocalyptic lineal view of history has here resulted in an isolation which permits only a negative attitude and action toward the world. Current history is given up and hope exists only for the end when God's wrath toward the world will be more in evidence than his mercy.[1]

Yet it must be emphasized that such a viewpoint, developed and continued in persecution, dominates neither the Old nor the New Testaments. Much more characteristic is the emphasis of the Old Testament prophets which is likewise central in Jesus and Paul. For Second Isaiah (Chaps. 40–55), for example, the clue to history and to the place of the elect community within history is to be discovered in the identity and nature of God. He is not one who has quit his active sovereignty until such a time as a demonic history has run down its full and predictable course. Rather he is the active Lord of time, the Creator and Redeemer of Israel. He is Lord now, and thus is known as Creator at the beginning. His activity is never ceasing; he is powerful and tireless, always at work, the first and the last to be sure, but at the same time all between. Hence the world runs in a course that is not entirely predictable. Society is not a part of the order of creation; there is no universal law of a static kind, no immutable structure in the heavens which is the prototype of things earthly. Only God is immutable, but he is always active. He has his plan, but he is engaged now in new creative acts. He is the God who creates 'the new thing'. His redemptive activity now is his eschatological activity, and this activity is within the current

[1] It should be said, however, that I John is a letter about internal conditions. It does not deny that the Church is to witness; in fact, the author would probably have affirmed it. Yet he, like the other authors in the New Testament, would have offered no hope for a society not centred in Christ. Since the New Testament writers did not look for the complete conversion of all mankind without divine judgment, they did not envisage social Utopia in the future apart from severe purging.

course of history. For this reason, the future is always open, and God's people are called to responsible activity in and for the world now. God has not seceded from history, giving it over to other powers until such a time as he sees fit again to intervene'

Apocalypticism developed between Second Isaiah and the opening pages of the New Testament. The latter had its deep influence upon the New Testament, but the main source of inspiration in the latter was the God of the fathers and of the prophets who in Jesus Christ had wrought the new thing expected of old. Here again is the active God who preserves an open history, who has made the *new* covenant, the *new* life, the *new* creation; and who creates in the believer an immediate expectancy, immediate but nevertheless inclusive of the whole future.

It may be remarked at this point that biblical hope is a problem to the modern Church, not simply because of the apocalyptic dress which it occasionally assumes, but primarily because the active Lord who creates an expectancy for the 'new thing' no longer dominates the Church's faith. In the New Testament, however, God *has come* in Jesus Christ, whom he has raised from the dead. Love, flowing from the love of God, is poured into our hearts through the Holy Spirit (Rom. 5.5). Hence we are constrained to hope; we are saved by hope; and the hope is for what we do not see but for which we wait with patience (Rom. 8.24–25). This hope is concerned with the whole creation now in bondage to decay, so that both it and we groan in travail while awaiting redemption. Yet the first fruits of the Spirit are in our midst and we know that nothing can separate us from the love of God as shown in Christ. In Chapter 8 of Romans the Apostle Paul is thus able to present hope apart from its apocalyptic dress and apart from the apocalyptic notion of a world grown old and feeble, rushing towards its abyss, while the elect await a 'cataclysmic

deliverance to a Utopian world of anthropomorphic bliss
(II Ezra 14.9–18; 5.51–54; Baruch 85.10). 'Paul's hope is neither
the radical cure from the radical physical and moral ills of
the world (apocalyptic), nor the extension of confidence in its
physical and moral potentialities for relative progress to
perfection (modern progress philosophy), nor the result of
boredom with a world which always is what it is. It is a hope
against such hopes (Rom. 4.18), a hope in things invisible to
human eyes, transcending human understanding (Rom. 8.25);
a hope based on the God who was in Christ, who is able to do
what he has promised (Rom. 4.21; 15.8–13).'[1] For this reason,
complete pessimism regarding the world, which releases the
called community from responsibility to withdrawal, is not
possible. God has not withdrawn himself, but is able and will
do 'signs and wonders' for which we must diligently look and
expectantly wait. Our responsibility is thus here in this
life now, and there must be no evasion of it.

2. Tendencies toward withdrawal occasionally took form
in a variety of ascetic practices. For the most part, we hear of
such practices achieving elaborate forms only during the second
and following centuries of the Christian era, though part
of their rootage can be traced back into the biblical period.
They were concerned with self-denial in food, drink, sexual
relations and material comforts. The Ebionites, the Thera-
putae of Egypt as described by Philo, the Gnostic sects, and the
Montanists, among many others, all practised forms of
self-denying and world-renouncing asceticism. The Gnostics

[1] These words and the thought contained in the preceding two
paragraphs are from an unpublished paper of Paul Schubert, 'Contemporary Relevance of Biblical Eschatology', presented before the
Theological Discussion Group, meeting in Washington, D.C.,
November 7–9, 1952. The paper was in part a warning against the
assumption, so frequently made, that apocalyptic eschatology is the
norm by which biblical eschatology is to be interpreted.

Valentinus and Marcion during the second century, for example, espoused both virginity and vegetarianism, the latter involving also the rejection of wine and stong drink. Yet it must be noted that such ascetic practices received much of their impetus, not from the Bible, but from the pagan world of the time. This was a world dominated by Hellenistic dualism of flesh versus spirit, whence it was inferred that severe bodily discipline and abstinence were the ways to liberate the soul to its proper function. Vegetarianism was early advocated by the Pythagorean and Orphic schools of thought and was widely spread throughout the ancient world. Its ultimate source is to be found there rather than in the Bible.[1] Sex as an evil thing to be denied expression is likewise a derivative from the conception of the physical as the source of sin, though its ultimate source may perhaps be found in more ancient notions of ritual purification and abstinence before approaching deity (note, e.g., I Sam. 21.4–5).

In any case, ascetic views regarding food and sex appeared in the New Testament Church, and the praise of virginity seems definitely to be given in Rev. 14.4. Yet basic biblical views concerning the goodness of all that God created, and the unitary view of man which interpreted sin as an act of will rather than as the natural expression of the material or physical nature, prevented any writer from giving full approval to asceticism. To be sure, the strictest personal discipline is required of any follower of Christ to the end that he 'keep himself unspotted from the world' (James 1.27). To be joined to Christ should make it impossible to join one's body

[1] See, for example, Ernst von Dobschütz, *Christian Life in the Primitive Church* (tr. by George Bremmer, ed. by W. D. Morrison), London and New York, 1904, pp. 126–8, 396–9; and M. M. Deems, 'The Sources of Christian Ascetism', *Environmental Factors in Christian History* (ed. by J. T. McNeill, Matthew Spinka, and H. R. Willoughby), Chicago, 1939, pp. 149–66 with references there cited.

with a harlot; as the temple of the Holy Spirit the body is to be kept pure (I Cor. 6.15–20). Yet there is no evil in food, drink or sex in themselves, unless they become expressions of lust (e.g. Mark 7.15–23). The Apostle Paul's abstinence from marriage was not motivated by any notions regarding the sinfulness of sex, but, as he says, solely by a concern that one should be as unencumbered as possible 'in view of the impending distress' (I Cor. 7.26; R.S.V.). The time is very short, he said, and we must be anxious about the affairs of the Lord rather than about the affairs of this world. Yet such remarks, he continues, should not lay any restraint upon those who hear them. They are meant solely to secure undivided devotion to the Lord. If one wishes to marry, he is to do so. If married, sexual abstinence (such as that practised by later Gnostics) is not to be encouraged, unless as a temporary arrangement by mutual agreement in order that the couple may devote themselves to a season of prayer (I Cor. 7.4–5). Sex is not an evil, and abstinence has no value in itself to purify the soul; the virgin is no purer than the one married.

According to Rom. 14 we infer that there were those in the Church at Rome who abstained from the eating of meat and the drinking of wine, while others did not. The difference of opinion on the vegetarian question had evidently caused considerable dissension. In this instance the Apostle endeavours to quiet the argument by persuading Christians to respect the opinions of one another, to do nothing 'for the sake of food' so as to destroy God's work, or to injure the faith of those with whom one disagrees. He insists only that everyone should have a clear reason, grounded in the faith, for what he does. Yet it is also clear that Paul thinks of vegetarianism as an unimportant thing in itself, and its acceptance as the act of a weaker brother (14.2). Such a person is 'weak in faith' and he should be welcomed, though not in order to dispute his opinions. On another occasion, however, the Apostle points to the basic issue involved in external regulations of this sort: namely that of submitting to the world's legalism. If Christ has set the Christian free of 'the elemental spirits', there is no meaning to such regulations as 'Do not handle', 'Do not taste', 'Do not touch'. 'These have indeed an appearance of wisdom in promoting rigour of devotion and self-abasement and severity to the body, but they are of no value . . .' (Col. 2.23; R.S.V.). Perhaps the clearest statement of what might be considered the typical attitude of a biblical man of faith is to be found in I Tim. 4.1–4. This passage speaks of 'the pretensions of liars whose consciences are seared, who forbid marriage and enjoin abstinence from foods which God created to be received with thanksgiving by those who believe and know the truth. For everything created by God is good, and nothing is to be rejected if it is received with thanksgiving . . .' (R.S.V.). Tit. 1.15 is equally blunt: 'To the pure all things are pure, but to the corrupt and unbelieving nothing is pure' (R.S.V.).

In the Old Testament ascetic tendencies are to be observed only in the prophets Elijah and Jeremiah, in the Nazirite vow (Num. 6.1–8), and in the Rechabite brotherhood (Jer. 35). The lives of the first mentioned are to be explained simply as the necessity laid upon them according to their understanding of God's calling for them. Neither they nor John the Baptist commanded their followers to adopt a similar mode of living. The Nazirite vow to abstain from intoxicating drink and from cutting the hair was evidently taken for a certain period of time only,[1] during which a person was deemed 'holy to the Lord', having separated himself 'to the Lord'. On what occasions and for what reasons the vow was taken we are not

[1] So Num. 6. Samson, however, was separated from birth 'a Nazirite to God', evidently because his birth was a fulfilment of a special prayer (Judg. 13.2–5).

informed. The Rechabites were originally a Kenite tribe following the rules of an order established by their founder (I Chron. 2.55). They represented a thorough-going rebellion against settled life in 'civilized' agrarian society, in that they refused to live in houses and to drink wine. Instead, they preserved in the midst of Israel the simplicity of nomadic life. For both the Rechabites and Nazirites it seems probable that the vine had become a symbol of the evil of settled life in the land of Canaan. Yet it must be observed that they had no large following. The prophets did not espouse their cause, except to point out the evil designs of Israelites who would tempt them to forsake their vows (Amos 2.12), or, as in the case of Jeremiah (35), to use the Rechabite loyalty to their founder as a foil for demonstrating by contrast the faithlessness of Judeans to their God.[1]

[1] The Jewish Covenanters and Essenes of late pre-Christian and early Christian times, from among whom John the Baptist may have come, had withdrawn from participation in the on-going Jewish life of the time to a type of monastic existence. A large colony of them lived in the wilderness of Judea at the north-west corner of the Dead Sea. Their primary reason for withdrawal was to give themselves more rigorously to the study of the Mosaic law because, they believed, Jewish life and Jewish leaders had betrayed the faith and there was nothing for them to do but to withdraw and form new communities. As far as we know, asceticism of the Hellenistic type played no prominent role in their life and thought. To be sure, many of the Essenes renounced marriage, though others including the Covenanters did not. Nevertheless, their ascetic withdrawal is perhaps better illustrated by the lives of an Elijah or a John the Baptist than by the later Gnostic asceticism, the roots of which were definitely in Hellenistic rather than in biblical conceptions. See further William H. Brownlee, 'A Comparison of the Covenanters of the Dead Sea Scrolls with the Pre-Christian Jewish Sects,' *The Biblical Archaeologist*, Vol. XIII, No. 3, Sept. 1950; and Miller Burrows, 'The Discipline Manual of the Judaean Covenanters', *Oudtestamentische Studiën*, Deel VIII (ed. by P. A. H. De Boer), Leiden, 1950, pp. 156–92.

C. Participation in Economic Life

Biblical thought concerning the active God who demanded of his community an active participation in the world's life, and whose creation was not evil in its physical nature, is to be seen as the dominant ideology governing the life of the community within the world. We have observed tendencies in the opposite direction, but they were conditioned by a variety of factors which did not control or dominate the community as a whole. We may now observe certain economic and geographical facts which must be noted before further theological generalizations can be made.

1. The first is the obvious fact that the new society was a comparatively small one, surrounded by a vast sea of paganism in which it was compelled to live. Economic self-sufficiency was a virtual impossibility. Because Palestine lacks an abundant natural wealth, it was in antiquity simply a poor suburb, economically, of Syria to which it is geographically tied. To live in such a country meant of necessity a close association with the surrounding world. This situation was accentuated by political factors. Foreign rulers opened the door to a dangerous cultural and religious accommodation, which puppet governments were usually glad to foster in order to allay sources of tension. The rapid hellenization of Palestine, beginning as early as the fifth century B.C., is the most spectacular case in point. Two small items are illustrative among many others: the introduction of coinage into the Persian Empire, modelled after Greek practice, brought a radical change in monetary matters, while the new and economical Greek lamp was soon imitated by all local potters who for centuries changed their styles in keeping with those currently made in Athens and Corinth. The architectural styles and programmes of the Hellenistic and Roman periods

142

were foreign importations. Herod the Great, for example, turned certain cities, notably Caesarea, Samaria, Jerusalem and Jericho, from Asiatic to Hellenic within a comparatively few years. The course of time brought the hippodrome and the theatre for the enjoyment of an increasingly large hellenized segment of the population.

Israel's dependence upon and accommodation · to the economic and cultural world were equally significant, even though not always as spectacular. In material culture Israel contributed little or nothing to its world, but borrowed virtually everything. Changes in the styles of Syrian pottery vessels were soon reflected in all Palestinian shops. From the ninth to the sixth centuries B.C. pottery was functional and standardized to such an extent that it testifies to mass production methods, probably introduced from Phoenicia. Clothing, jewelry, cosmetics and the like all called for special industries which faithfully followed the fashions of the day. On the Black Obelisk of the Assyrian emperor, Shalmaneser III (859–824 B.C.), Israelites are shown wearing the same clothing as men from Northern Syria and Southern Armenia, though differing from that worn by those from the southern and eastern portions of the empire. Life in Jerusalem and Samaria during the tenth and ninth centuries B.C. must have been almost as cosmopolitan as that in Tyre, a city then becoming one of the chief commercial centres of the world. Envoys and traders came in large numbers from numerous countries. Indeed, the very word 'Canaanite' came to be used as a term for a foreign 'trader' (e.g. Prov. 31.24; Zech. 14.21), so familiar were Israelites with Canaanite merchants in their midst. The far-flung economic exploits of Solomon, including his control of trade from South Arabia and the Somaliland, his position as middleman for horses from Cilicia and chariots from Egypt, his great expansion of Israel's metallurgical industry, etc., are all well known. So also is the rapid development of a wealthy 'middle class' of traders in Israelite society which gravely threatened the older equalitarian social structure.[1]

2. Now what was to be done in such a situation? The purist attempt at complete withdrawal, as illustrated in the Rechabite movement, never won over the majority, even of the men of faith. Biblical man, especially in the Old Testament, set great value upon the good things of earth which God had provided for man's enjoyment. Hence economic life, which is the system of arrangements whereby these good things are secured and distributed, could no more be looked upon as evil in itself than could the goods themselves. Material abundance was seen as an evil in two situations only: (a) when it led members of the community to a denial of their dependence upon and obedience to their Lord; and (b) when it was gained at the expense and impoverishment of the weaker neighbour.

Israelite law furnished no barrier to international trade. In Israel loans were usually to alleviate poverty. No interest was to be charged on such loans because the need of a brother in the community should not be an occasion for profit. Yet interest could be charged on foreign loans, which were usually connected with business relations (Deut. 23.19–20). In both Testaments the right of individuals to own property was assumed, but there was a higher law than the right of private ownership. In Israel the ultimate sanction for the disposal of property was in the hands of the family or clan. It was considered God's loan, and as such could not be used for speculation in which the weak and poor could be defrauded. Hence Divine ownership and clan control served the purpose of protecting the interests of the weak and preserving an equalitarian status for the members of the community. Yet

[1] See further, e.g. W. F. Albright, *The Archaeology of Palestine*, Pelican Books, A 199, 1949, especially Chap. 9.

the increasing pressures caused by the concentration of economic power in the hands of those who were newly rich, largely because of international trade, threatened to disrupt the older order. And government was forced to be tolerant because of its dependence upon the wealthy for the taxation needed to support its architectural and military programmes. The older law, devised for a simpler agrarian economy, was easily subverted by legalistic means so that its intention was disregarded even when the system as a whole was given formal adherence. Debt slavery increased, but we have no record of the old law of release, contained in Exod. 21.2–6, being used to check it.[1]

This was the situation which Israel's pre-Exilic prophets faced. They attacked it, not by condemning business life as such, or even international trade, but by giving a renewed call to loyalty. Their primary concern was with obedience to God's intention, and they attacked all forms of hair-splitting legalism which appeared to give formal justification to current compromise (e.g. Jer. 2.8; 7.21–23; 8.8). To them idolatry and injustice went hand in hand. The tolerance born of international contact bred idolatry in the prophetic sense; and, when the demand of God for absolute obedience from his people was in any degree softened, the intention of the covenant law was easily set aside. Thus the prophetic attack was upon the idolatry of both the prosperous and the compromisers who by accommodation tried to find their security. There was no real principle remaining in either group. Both

[1] For more detailed analysis of the question of property in Israel, see Walter Eichrodt, 'The Question of Property in the Light of the Old Testament', *Biblical Authority for Today* (ed. by Alan Richardson and W. Schweitzer), London and Philadelphia, 1951, pp. 257–74; and C. L. Taylor, 'Old Testament Foundations', *Christianity and Property* (ed. by J. F. Fletcher), Philadelphia, 1947, pp. 11–30.

easily misused their economic power, adding house to house and field to field till there was no room in the land for any but themselves (Isa. 5.8).

If the prophets did not present a detailed plan for proper economic life in the world, it was because they believed that God already had done so in the covenant law. There God's intention was fully expressed; his people were to constitute a brotherhood, each possessing equal rights and equal access to economic security. The law was filled with safeguards to protect the weak so that they might not be pressed down into an inferior status in which responsible community life could no longer be their portion. The dignity of responsible citizenship in God's commonwealth and of God's blessing in material goods was the right of all and the promise of the covenant order. Yet, said the prophets, the strong have betrayed the order and rebelled against God; for this reason, God will destroy the community and take away its property.

The knowledge of God's intention thus prevented the prophets from taking the simplest course open to them: namely, complete withdrawal from 'civilized' and increasingly complicated business life. Instead, they pointed to the tension between people and God, called sin by its proper name, and rehearsed the fundamentals of the covenant faith. To live in the world meant a considerable risk; it involved the knowledge of God's judgment, of his 'Day' upon all the proud and haughty, of the danger of losing all to find anything.

The New Testament does not furnish us with sufficient material to enable us to say very much about the economic life of Christians in the world. They gained their living by working among pagans even as did the Jews. Like the Israelites of old the dominant attitude of most of them was neither complete renunciation nor acceptance. The so-called 'communism' of the early community in Jerusalem has often been misinterpreted. It was not a complete programme for the life of all Christians, but actually a means to alleviate poverty. The gospel appealed at first to few rich people, and there were many poor in the economically parasitic city of Jerusalem. The common life of the disciples with Jesus had instilled in them a generous spirit, and this type of life was now extended as a means of caring for the poor (Acts 4.32–37).

It was generally expected that a Christian would continue in the work he had been doing before he was converted. Paul worked along with the people and he encouraged others to do the same so that they be a burden to no one (e.g. I Thess. 4.9–12; II Thess. 3.6–13). Barnabas sold a field and was especially commended because he gave the money to the Jerusalem community (Acts 4.36–37). Others did not dispose of property and were not expected to do so unless they wished. They were expected to stay where they were and do nothing to upset the present order until Christ came again. Inasmuch as no class or economic distinctions exist in God's sight, Christians were to be patient with their current situations until the warfare of God is complete (e.g. James 5.7–11). Slaves were to stay in service, being submissive, kind and gentle, even to overbearing masters, remembering that in following Christ's example the innocent who suffer will be blessed of God (I Pet. 2.18–25). In other words, the slave was to be a good slave, serving 'in singleness of heart, fearing the Lord' (Col. 4.22; Eph. 6.5–8). Masters on their part were to treat their slaves in Christian love, remembering that both have a Master in whom there is no partiality (Eph. 6.9; Col. 4.4). Earthly distinctions in status receive no permanent validation from the heavenly throne.

This means that the New Testament envisions no revolutionary upset in the economic order which is to be brought about by Christians. God himself would bring about the revolution and the non-political community of the New Testament was not a coercive instrument. The Church was instead to live humbly in love, with patient expectation, acting as a leaven within the evil institutions of the world. The first thing to be done for pagan man was to convert him. If, once he were within the community, he needed help, he would receive it, for the economic obligation of Christians to one another was very keen indeed. This was not the sole obligation of Christians, as the parable of the good Samaritan shows, but it indicates the concentration of Christian energy and thought.

On the other hand, however, the New Testament is as much concerned as the Old with all practices which oppress the poor. In the teaching of Jesus and in the Epistles there is a constant stream of criticism directed at the misuse of money (e.g. the parable of the rich man and Lazarus, Luke 16.19–31; and the parable of the rich fool, Luke 12.13–21). Indeed, it must be said that a dominant biblical theme is a radical criticism of economic injustice which works hardship and suffering on the poor. For this reason, Christians are to be especially concerned with a heavenly rather than with an earthly treasure (Luke 12.33–34). They are to beware of covetousness and a love of money which is the root of all evils (Col. 3.5; I Tim. 6.9–10; James 5.1–6). Those who enter the new community in possession of wealth are not to be haughty or 'to set their hopes on uncertain riches but on God who richly furnishes us with everything to enjoy. They are to do good, to be rich in good deeds, liberal and generous, thus laying up for themselves a good foundation for the future, so that they may take hold of the life which is life indeed' (I Tim. 6.17–19; R.S.V.).

D. Participation in Political and Cultural Life

1. The Christian attitude toward the Roman State varied in the New Testament, ranging from absolute condemnation to approval and co-operation. Both extremes seem to be present in every period,[1] and it is doubtful whether any Christian felt the need to harmonize them, even though in times of persecution he may have felt most strongly the Satanic character of the state. The reasons for this dual attitude have been discussed in Chapter II and need not be repeated here. The sovereignty of God over all history meant that 'Herod and Pontius Pilate with the Gentiles and the peoples of Israel' were gathered against 'thy holy servant Jesus . . . to do whatever thy hand and thy plan had predestined to take place' (Acts 4.25–28). Jesus recognized the role of Cæsar and repudiated revolution, while Paul said that obedience should be given to the powers. Thus the nations are the unconscious instruments of the divine judgment, and submission is due them. The judgment that is forbidden to the community of believers is performed by the state (Rom. 12.19), which exists for their good and for wrath upon the wrongdoer (Rom. 13.3–5; I Pet. 2.14). Hence prayers for kings, rulers and all in high places are urged upon the community (I Tim. 2.1–2).[2]

[1] For example, in approximately the same time that Revelation pictures the Roman Empire as a Satanic beast or blasphemous harlot in which there is no positive value, Clement of Rome composes a beautiful prayer for political rulers in which he says: 'Give them, Lord, health, peace, concord, stability, in order that they may administer without offence the government that has been given them by thee' (I Clement 61.1–2).

[2] In a similar situation Jeremiah urged the same policy upon the Judean exiles in Babylonia (Jer. 29.7).

Nevertheless, state and nations have no ultimate status and their authority is limited. Though Jesus gives recognition to Cæsar he talks depreciatingly of the princes of the world, speaks contemptuously of those who call themselves 'benefactors', and calls Herod a fox because of his conniving cruelty (Luke 12.32). Jesus relativizes the claim of the earthly ruler because it is God alone who is Lord, and 'Render unto Cæsar' becomes subordinate to the relation, 'Render unto God'. This very relativizing is further indicated when it is urged that the disciples must not lord it over one another, as the rulers of the Gentiles do, but must live as servants of one another (Mark 10.42–45). According to Paul the rulers of this world are to pass away (I Cor. 2.6) and the Christians are to *judge* the world and the angels (I Cor. 6.2). These powers or the state through which they rule are divine agents, but they have overstepped their role (I Cor. 2.8) and have become agents enslaving man. It is for this reason that Christians must not only judge the world, but they must not submit their disputes to the judgment of unbelievers, for lawsuits are a disgrace for them (I Cor. 6.4–6). The called community possesses the means of ultimate judgment. They even rule, having become kings, though Paul has to add sarcastically to the Christians: 'Would that you did reign'; that is, would that they had learned of their kingship rather than having quarrelled over which leader they should follow! (I Cor. 4.8; cf. II Tim. 2.12; Rev. 5.6–10).

The Christian responsibility of judgment, of 'reigning' as kings in the world, involves an active, positive and responsible role in the world's life,[1] one which creates and sustains a tension between state and community. It is characteristic of

[1] This attitude, as previously indicated, is not uniformly present in all writings; it appears to be entirely absent, for example, from the Epistles of John.

the former to resist criticism, while it is incumbent upon the latter to give it, precisely because its first allegiance to its Lord furnishes it with the means of ultimate judgment. As to when the state should be opposed, no rules are given. In both Testaments decision is left to the individual member of the community as a part of his responsible service to the Lord. Paul certainly knew of at least one occasion when the political authority could be opposed when he escaped from Damascus in a basket (II Cor. 11.32). Acts records cases of imperial abuse in the experience of Paul when the magistrates acted unjustly at Philippi (16.22–24), when Festus sought the favour of the Jewish leaders (25.9), when Felix hoped for a bribe (24.26), and when Gallio, while he would not prosecute unjustly, would not protect the Christians from unjust persecution (18.12–16). For the state to fail in the procedures of justice and order was grounds to oppose it because it had removed itself from its God-willed service. The time for criticism and disobedience is when the state usurps the divine authority and puts itself forth as the final arbiter of life and destiny. The experience of Peter and John before the authorities reflects the same ground of resistance (Acts 4). Obedience is due the civil power only so long as it has not rebelled against the divine authority. Not even silence can be maintained, for the Christian must give voice to what he has seen and heard of God's activity.

In the Old Testament the most vivid parallel to the responsible citizenship of the Christian is the figure of the prophet. His ringing challenge that the day is at hand when one must choose for God or against him, and his role as interpreter of all earthly events, his ability to hold all nations before the bar of divine requirement and judgment, are a barrier against quiescence and the illustration of a responsibility laid before each member of the new community. Natural religion had then and still has as one of its notable characteristics the attempt to do away with the tension between the divine and the human in order that society may find its secure integration in the rhythm of cosmic life. The result is the elevation of certain human institutions, notably state and cultus, in order to give them divine sanction and a permanence of divine rank. The proclamation of the prophet, however, destroys every such human pretension in order to make clear the relativity of all human structures of power in the light of God's revealed order.

In the New Testament the form of resistance was for the most part oral. If this got one into trouble with the authorities, the example of Christ should and did lead to dignified submission. In the cases of Stephen, Peter and Paul spirited defence was also given, and sincere effort was made to turn the occasion into one in which God and the gospel were glorified. In the Old Testament prophetic resistance was likewise oral, and only once were the prophetic energies employed to lead and encourage a violent and bloody political revolution, namely that of Jehu against the Dynasty of Omri (I Kings 17–11 Kings 10). In this extreme case, however, the whole basis of the new society was threatened when royal power was used to introduce Baal of Tyre as head of the state in place of the Lord of Israel. In the covenant theology such an attempt was the ultimate act of political blasphemy (cf. Deut. 13); and there is no more dramatic story in all literature than the spirited and courageous stand of the Prophet Elijah against Ahab and Jezebel. Nevertheless, the extreme violence of the revolution was later repudiated, if we are to judge from the reference in Hosea 1.4, and that type of violence was never again employed as an instrument of policy. Or, at least, we may say that no comparable situation again arose until the Maccabean revolt against Antiochus Epiphanes in the second century B.C.[1] We should observe, however, that the prophets possessed a keen sense of timing in their acts of oral resistance. The evidence suggests that they spoke most vigorously at critical moments in the affairs of state, and always in a dramatic manner on occasions when their words would secure the widest hearing and dissemination.[2]

2. A further proof of the positive, rather than purely negative, attitude of the biblical community to the world is to been seen in the area of cultural accommodation. In general, it may be said that there was the greatest freedom in borrowing from surrounding culture, and tension arose over such borrowing only when it threatened the basis of community faith or when its re-interpretation in the biblical setting was too slow to keep pace with the deepening of insight into the implications of the faith. On the other hand, resistance to cultural accommodation seems to have been strongest in those

[1] The policies of those subsequent kings to whom the form and substance of religion were largely matters of political policy (notably those of Manasseh, II Kings 22.1–16) were far more subtle than the policy of Jezebel. They involved the worship of various pagan deities and the introduction of numerous pagan practices under the guise of Yahwism, without disturbing Yahweh's place at the head of the national religion. In this way, the faith of Israel could easily have been converted into another polytheism, with Yahweh at the head of a pantheon of divine beings, each of whom could possess his or her own cultus. See further G. Ernest Wright, *The Old Testament Against its Environment*, London and Chicago, 1950, pp. 30–41.

[2] That is, especially on festival occasions when large numbers of people would be present. Jeremiah, as is well known, had to remain in hiding during much of the reign of Jehoiakim. His datable prophecies group themselves around certain occasions: (1) the first year of Jehoiakim in 608 B.C., (2) after the victory of Nebuchadnezzar in 605, (3) the first revolt in 598, (4) the planned revolt in 594–3, and (5) the second revolt in 589–7. The prophetic Word was not scattered indiscriminantly.

times when community vitality was at its lowest ebb and every effort was expended simply to preserve the traditions and to encourage a keen consciousness of distinctiveness (e.g. in the Post-Exilic period of the Old Testament).

The clearest illustrations of direct borrowing appear in Israelite poetry. Some of its forms, at least, were taken over directly from Canaanite literature, including metre and a climatic or repetitive rhetorical structure. The Psalter is now known to swarm with words, phrases and allusions which were taken from the works of Canaanite poets. Psalm 29, for example, has been shown to be fundamentally Canaanite in diction and imagery; it was probably adapted by an Israelite poet from a hymn to Baal.[1] The material in the Book of Proverbs is another vivid example of cultural accommodation. Such proverbs arose within a 'wisdom' movement in which no tension existed between Israelite, Egyptian, Canaanite, Edomite and other adherents to the epigrammatic teaching of prudential ethics. While in Israel the theological basis of wisdom became 'the fear of the Lord', the proverbs nevertheless were drawn for the most part from an international movement concerned with the character education of the individual. Even the poems in praise of personified wisdom (Prov. 8–9) possess close parallels elsewhere, particularly in Canaanite literature. So close are the proverbs to the international sources whence they were derived that they are lacking almost completely in the typically Israelite conception of society as described in Chapter III. For this reason their doctrine of divine reward and punishment is confined to the individual, and this issued in a sharp scepticism of the whole basis of

[1] In support of these generalizations, see e.g. J. H. Patton, *Canaanite Parallels in the Book of Psalms*, Baltimore, 1944; and W. F. Albright, 'The Psalm of Habakkuk', *Studies in Old Testament Prophecy* (ed. by H. H. Rowley), Edinburgh, 1950, pp. 1–18.

wisdom (cf. Job and Eccles.). This conflict was only resolved in the intertestamental period when wisdom, law, word and eschatology were brought together in such a way that the scepticism of Job and Ecclesiastes played no further role.[1] It is indeed a matter of considerable interest that the biblical community could accommodate itself to a purely prudential ethic, while at the same time it retained a more radical ethic, in which shrewd calculation was distinctly secondary, if not excluded.

Further illustrations are so numerous that we can mention only a few. The sacrificial system of worship required considerable reinterpretation in the Israelite setting, though even then it did not cease entirely to be a problem.[2] The institution of kingship was acknowledged to be a direct borrowing from pagan society (e.g. I Sam. 8.4) but in Israel the intepretation of the office had to be acclimatized to the community faith. 'If kingship counted in Egypt as a function of the gods, and in Mesopotamia as a divinely ordained political order, the Hebrews knew that they had introduced it on their own initiative, in imitation of others and under the strain of an emergency. . . . Kingship never achieved a standing equal to that of institutions which were claimed—rightly or wrongly—to have originated during the Exodus and the desert wandering.'[3] In spite of the strong pretensions of the royal theology, fostered in the Jerusalem Court, equally strong suspicions of it remained, so that in the reconstruction of the New Jerusalem contained in Ezek. 40–48 the term 'king' was abandoned

[1] Cf. J. Coert Rylaarsdam, *Revelation in Jewish Wisdom Literature*, Chicago, 1946; and G. Ernest Wright, *God Who Acts*, London and Chicago, 1952, pp. 102–5.

[2] Cf., for example, Ps. 50 and Acts 17; see further G. Ernest Wright, *The Old Testament Against its Environment*, Chap. III.

[3] Henri Frankfort, *Kingship and the Gods*, Chicago, 1948, pp. 339–40.

entirely for the political leader.[1] It survived nonetheless, but in eschatological dress, and the kingship of the risen Christ was seen by the early Church as its fulfilment and inner significance. Similarly, the Solomonic Temple as in some manner an abode of deity, a 'house of God', was a foreign importation which required reinterpretation in Israel, but which like kingship never became an indispensable institution of community life, important though it was conceived to be.[2] And, finally, we may mention the familiar problem of death and the after-life. Israelite Sheol as the abode of the dead represented views essentially similar to those held in Syria and Mesopotamia, though differing sharply from Egyptian beliefs. To be sure, Sheol was stripped of much of its polytheistic mythology in Israel, but it was one arena which the faith of Israel was slowest to penetrate. Only at the end of the Old Testament period does the doctrine of resurrection make its appearance (Isa. 26.19; Dan. 12.2); and while there continued to be those who retained the older views (e.g. the Sadducees), yet for the majority of Jews the faith in God's redemptive power had finally won its victory over death.

Needless to say, the world of New Testament times was exceedingly complex, characterized as it was by the fluid mixture of Hellenistic and ancient Near Eastern conceptions. The points of contact between this world and that of the New Testament community are so manifold and intricate that it is impossible even to summarize them here. For our purposes it is important only to note the viable and positive relation

[1] Cf. Martin Noth, *Das System der Zwölf Stämme Israels*, Stuttgart, 1930, pp. 151–62.

[2] Cf. Jer. 7. See also the symposium by Harold H. Nelson, A. Leo Oppenheim, G. Ernest Wright and Floyd V. Filson, 'The Significance of the Temple in the Ancient Near East', *The Biblical Archaeologist*, Vol. VII, 1944, pp. 41–88.

existing between this new people and their environment. The Apostle Paul could borrow the form of the Cynic diatribe and take over as well secular terms from the moral vocabulary of the Stoics, using them for his own purpose. It is possible also that he adopted expressions and even viewpoints which originated among the so-called 'mystery' religions of the time. It is doubtful that he was so much influenced by them as that he simply made use of them for his own purposes in the Gentile world.[1] On the other hand, there were terms like 'immortality' which he seems consciously to have avoided because there were limits set by their original setting which precluded his use of them. The evangelist John in employing the Greek term *logos* for the Word which was co-existent with God and had now become flesh (John I) exhibited an extraordinary theological accommodation to his environment, reinterpreting the conception in Christian terms. On the one hand, the use of the term would immediately recall to those trained in Greek philosophy a wealth of context on which entirely new light was now shed. On the other hand, for Eastern readers the concept of the personified divine Word had had a long history in the Semitic world. Indeed, the conception, as John uses it, has its closest kinship with Judaeo-Hellenistic literature and behind that with two millennia of usage in the Near East.[2] Yet this divine, creative word of long history was now focused in the person of Christ.

Many more indirect and unconscious effects of the climate of the age upon the new community are to be observed in the

[1] Cf. the careful and sober treatment of this subject, one about which many unbalanced statements have been made, by A. D. Nock, *St. Paul*, London, 1938, especially pp. 77ff.

[2] See L. Durr, *Die Wertung des göttlichen Wortes im Alten Testament und im antiken Orient*, Leipzig, 1938; and W. F. Albright, *From the Stone Age to Christianity*, Baltimore, 1940, pp. 285–6.

increased complexity of the divine world. Pre-Christian Judaism, engaged as it was with 'building a fence' around the holiness of God, so emphasized the divine transcendence that the way was cleared to fill the intermediate area between God and his world with a host of lesser beings (cf. Gnosticism's emanations), including the semi-hypostatizing or personalizing of such terms as Wisdom, Word and Presence. Common features which Judaism had with Iranian religion may have led to influence from that quarter in the further development of these features: e.g. the increasing tendency toward dualism and the developing conception of Satan, the elaboration of a mythology of angels with the separation and identification of seven archangels, and the developing belief in a last judgment and of rewards or punishments meted out after death. In any event, Satan brought with him a segment of the polytheistic world of demonology, so that the New Testament world is one which is filled with the principalities and powers of darkness.

Yet a partial reaction against this world is to be observed in the fact that the Christian community of the first century is singularly free of elaborate mythological speculation concerning angels and demons, as well as of the astrology and magic which tended to accompany them. For example, faith healing and not incantation fills the pages of the New Testament. Faith in Christ was power over the spirits of darkness. The simplicity and directness of Christ's teaching brought with it also a recovery of Israel's faith in the immediate sovereignty and activity of God, a factor which in Israel had prevented the development of a mythology of intermediate beings. A living faith requires a living God, and whenever the fundamental biblical proclamation concerning his immediate and active Lordship over present history is neglected, a variety of intermediate substitutes will be introduced,

A curious blend of Hellenic and Semitic elements appears in Gnosticism, a highly sophisticated and somewhat esoteric movement which developed over the centuries in both pagan and Christian dress. The earliest Gnostic known to Irenaeus and Hippolytus was Simon Magus, who in Acts 8.9–13 is said to have been converted by Philip; and there was certainly a proto-gnosticism in existence long before the developed forms known to the Church Fathers had been evolved. The precise influence which certain elements in Gnosticism had upon the New Testament community is a subject of debate which cannot be settled until we possess a more detailed and chronological knowledge of what the movement was in its earliest phases.[1] Such clear references as we have, however, certainly suggest the condemnation of those Christians who were accommodating themselves to the movement. I John is concerned throughout with the contrast between true and false knowledge; Timothy is warned against the godless chatter and contradictions of those who falsely claim to possess knowledge (*gnosis*; I Tim. 6.20); the Colossian Church was warned against those who claimed superior knowledge, paid great regard to angels and taught asceticism (Col. 2.8, 18, 21–23); and in Section B of this chapter we have already indicated the Christian reaction to an asceticism based upon Hellenic views regarding the dualism of spirit and matter.

The Fourth Gospel avoids the noun 'knowledge' and instead uses the active verb, 'knowing', with Christ, God and the message of the Church as objects. The Apostle Paul speaks of knowledge puffing up but of love building up (I Cor. 8.1). The

[1] For a discussion of the Semitic background of Gnosticism, see especially W. F. Albright, op cit., pp. 282–7. For important new information see also Victor R. Gold, 'The Gnostic Library of Chenoboskion', *The Biblical Archaeologist*, Vol. XV, No. 4, December 1952.

Church had no interest in aristocratic and esoteric knowledge.

Perhaps the most inportant thing to be said about New Testament literature, and particularly about the teaching of Jesus and Paul in the midst of such a complex world of ideas, is its originality, independence, and fine sense of balance and proportion.[1] Something to this effect must be meant by the oft-repeated statement that the new community lived in the world but not of it. We have seen that this cliché cannot be interpreted to mean complete withdrawal and complete rejection of the world. Instead it must mean that the community possessed the means of living within the world, in a positive relation to it, but with an independent judgment which enabled it both to reject and to affirm, while never losing the balance needed to preserve its own distinctiveness and inner power.

E. Conclusion

Finally, we must draw together some conclusions from the foregoing for the life of the individual member of the new community in the world.

1. First and foremost among these conclusions is the new dimension given to individuality. Conscious of the fact that he has been 'called out' of the world into the new community of the people of God, the individual now has before him the knowledge of the people's election to historical vocation; and, through the Holy Spirit, he is to find the calling set

[1] Albright, op. cit., p. 304 suggests that this sense of proportion, so foreign to contemporary Judaism, may itself represent a profound though indirect influence of Hellenism. The elaborate hermeneutics of Phariseeism, itself in a sense a Hellenic dialectic, was replaced, he suggests, by a far wider and deeper emphasis: Hellenistic universalism and philanthropy, which underlie the whole subsequent history of Christianity.

before him. He is placed in a society, but the mission of this society provides the context of his own mission. He is to live in and for the society's Lord, and in this covenanted service he discovers his true freedom and a summons to his highest capacities. Though he may be of small account in the eyes of the world, he can do 'signs and wonders' through the power of the Lord who sends him. On the one hand, he is bound 'in the bundle of life' of his people. On the other hand, he possesses a relationship of servant to his Lord, or of son to his Father, and the knowledge of the divine work and the divine 'thou shalt' set before him furnishes him with the means of independent existence and judgment. The call to love both the community's Lord and the neighbour indicates the dual and dependent relationship which he has in the world. He is both a responsible individual before God and a responsible segment of the community which exists in and by the Lord. Without the community he would have no place of standing, and without his calling to be worked out with fear and trembling before God and as a portion of the community's mission he would be lost in a social mass. This situation is paradoxical in the extreme except as it is viewed in a theocentric perspective. God as the community's Lord and as the active Lord of all history exercises his sovereignty now through Christ and through the Holy Spirit, and it is this sovereignty which binds the community into one 'body' and which also directs the life of the individual. Apart from this theocentricity, according to the biblical viewpoint, the social organism falls apart into self-deifying individuality which destroys true community, or it encloses the individual within it in such a way that he no longer will function as a responsible person with a responsible vocation (e.g. Ezek. 18.2, where the popular attitude is: 'The fathers have eaten sour grapes, and the children's teeth are set on edge').

While nourished and commissioned within the community, the individual nevertheless knows of the righteousness of God which has both formed and judged his people. Hence he is both loyal to the community and a critic of it. He is called to labour both for the purity of his people and for their true 'peace' because he knows of the existence of false prophets and of many adherents who will fall away in the Day of the Lord (e.g. Matt. 24.10–11). For this reason, not even the new community of God's people as it now exists in the world furnishes him with a perfectly secure place of refuge; his calling creates a tension which makes him alert to lurking dangers.

2. The scene of the calling for both the community and the individual within it is to be found *in* the world according to 'the state wherein we were called'. There can be no retreat from the world, for the divine election calls for a positive, rather than a negative relation to all those outside the community. God is Lord of the world and is engaged in the struggle to extend his sovereignty over it. The positive relationship which he requires of his people involves both acceptance and rejection of earthly culture and earthly masters. Our work is for the Lord, and our eye must be single. The motivation of decision must be derived from the singleness of our obedience. Earthly authorities of every type tend to insist that we observe rules and customs 'as means of salvation, as incentives for ambition and pride. But to obey any of them for such motives brings us again under bondage to the body of this death. To accept for ourselves the fears and hopes which they consider ultimate is to be enslaved by them. There is only one Master whom we are bound to serve (Matt. 6.24). Yet this Master commands us to remain in the state wherein we were called, obeying those who have been given authority over us. . . . On the other hand, when any earthly power

commands us to serve him and him alone, we cannot comply and at the same time be a servant of him who accepted the cross and despised the shame. The reconciling ministry of Jesus included both obedience to earthly authorities and refusal to serve them. And that is the ministry which his disciples share.'[1]

The community's obedience thus leaves the individual in a responsible relationship to the world here and now, for he is called upon continually to make decisions in keeping with his calling. To obey the divine Master in the earthly position wherein one is called thus involves a precarious type of existence in which choices and judgments must be made, but there is always danger of wrong decision. To avoid such danger it would appear that some form of radical withdrawal and completely negative rejection of the world would be the easiest and safest course. Yet this is precisely what is not permitted by the whole conception of election, unless as a purely temporary and tactical manoeuvre (as in the case of Jeremiah hiding from King Jehoiakim; see above note 2, p. 153).

The hazardous nature of the Christian's life is made the more acute because he is given no detailed rules on which he must base his decisions as he lives in the world. He is in possession of a revealed order made clear in the gospel proclaimed by the new community; he is bound in the *New Covenant* in Christ. This covenant possesses both a revealed and an inferential ethic, but it is not a legalistic system designed to protect the individual in all phases of his activity in the world. Its apodictic absolutes are impelling guides to decision, but their application is left to the individual and to such community decisions as may be made from time to time. Yet community interpretation and application does not carry the

[1] Paul S. Minear, 'The New Testament Witness and Civilization', *Theology Today*, Vol. V, 1948, pp. 347–8.

same authority as the divine Word in the revealed order. The tradition to be received, preserved and proclaimed (I Cor. 11.2; II Thess. 2.15; cf. Jude 3) has to do essentially with the *divine act* in Christ; it is no 'hedge' in the Jewish sense designed to *protect* the 'holiness' of God or the community, or to relieve the individual from the necessity of independent judgment. Yet the New Testament does not conceive of life in the world as entirely without guidance. The community has been given the gift of the Holy Spirit to strengthen, guide and lead it. The individual does not walk alone, for within the community the Spirit is active, extending the work of God in Christ (I Cor. 12.3). This does not provide the new society with a mysterious *gnosis* or knowledge which protects it from the world, but it does testify to the active sovereignty of the living God who would justify his people in the active protestation of their faith.

The biblical conception of the new society in the world as the bearer both of the divine promise and of the covenanted obligation correlates in a remarkable way the holy majesty of God with a fallen, sinful world; and it does so

'in a dramatic situation that is to unfold in time and is moving toward a future where the distant yet related parallels of human and divine existence are to meet in infinity. Not cosmic phenomena, but history itself, had here become pregnant with meaning. . . . The human being was not merely the servant [slave] of the god as he was in Mesopotamia; nor was he placed, as in Egypt, at a pre-ordained station in a static universe which did not need to be—and, in fact, could not be—questioned. Man . . . was the interpreter and the servant of God; he was even honored with the task of bringing about the realization of God's will. Thus . . . we find man possessed of a new freedom and

164

a new burden of responsibility. We also find there a new and utter lack of *eudaimonia*, of harmony—whether with the world of reason or with the world of perception.'[1]

These words well describe the situation of the biblical individual in the ancient world and give meaning to the almost strange poignancy to be observed in so many biblical people: Abraham at an altar with his son prepared for sacrifice, Moses and Jeremiah terrified by their calling, the lonely Elijah before an apostate nation, the exiles compelled to sing the Lord's song in a strange land (Ps. 137), Jesus deserted by his disciples and praying, 'Not my will but thine'. In the world as it now is the will of God is not be equated with *eudaimonia*, the love of God does not necessarily mean peace as men desire it, nor does the community of Christ provide a den of escape and safety from the turmoil. The elect are thrown into the world to follow wherever they are led, to lose in order to find, and to sacrifice harmony for a 'peace that passeth understanding'. Yet the strange fact is that this burden placed upon the individual is not heavy because he who himself is the Lord of the new community carries the burdens of those within it. The Head suffers with the body, and in his cross the precarious life of the individual is seen to be a means of divine reconciliation.

3. One of the reasons that the individual is enabled to exist creatively, though insecurely, in the world is because he can live without fear. And this is possible because he possesses a kingship, a means of judgment, a perspective and a knowledge concerning the present and future relation of the world to its true sovereignty.

For one thing, this knowledge enables him to interpret

[1] H. and H. A. Frankfort in *The Intellectual Adventure of Ancient Man*, Chicago, 1946, pp. 370–1.

civilization now and in the past as 'the society of men living according to man under the dominion of the fallen angels'.[1] This earthly society is characterized by a rejection of the light, a claim to greater rights than God intended, and an unwarranted trust in its own powers to erect controls and goals which are given the sanctity of a false ultimacy. Yet the dominion of Satan has been broken; the rebellion of men has been exposed; and a new society has been created. This society is composed of those whom God has delivered 'from the dominion of darkness' and has transferred 'to the kingdom of his beloved Son, in whom we have redemption and forgiveness of sins' (Col. 1.13–14). For this reason we are freed from all fundamental and ultimate fears regarding what the powers of darkness can do. The basic issue of sovereignty has been settled,[2] and we are freed from 'the illusions through which the demonic forces in a particular civilization claim for themselves a specious ultimacy'.[3]

Yet if no ultimate value is to be attached to the earthly society, if its structures of power, its claims and its promises possess in themselves no security or permanence, what is the meaning of the election of the new community in the world? If the revealed order is eschatological and, therefore, beyond current history as regards its consummation, why are we not simply required to separate ourselves both from the evil

[1] So Augustine, *City of God*, Book 16, Chap. 17—quoted by Paul L. Lehmann, 'The Bible and the Significance of Civilization', *Theology Today*, Vol. V, 1948, p. 350.

[2] The importance of this is made clear by the following definition of sovereignty, given by Paul L. Lehmann, *ibid.*, pp. 351–2: It is 'the authentic point of order in society, the point around which the basic patterns of thought and life are organized and sustained and at which the issue between meaningful unity and meaningless disunity is resolved'.

[3] Paul S. Minear, op. cit., p. 345.

and the struggle of current society? It is to be observed that both the prophets and the apostles believed that the end of the earthly societies would occur in the near future if it was not already at hand, and yet none of them gave up in any situation without an earnest struggle to fulfil their calling. God was at work, they knew, bringing salvation through the door of judgment, and they understood their primary calling to be the proclamation of God's sovereignty and the interpretation of the meaning of his acts. The elect were to do this, not through hope for material reward for themselves—though God's rewards are indeed a bountiful blessing—but simply because the Lord who formed the community was to be loved and obeyed and because the life of the elect discovered its sole meaning in the service to which they were called. The destiny of the individual is to be found when, and only when, the time of his life coincides with a segment of the election-time of the community, which in turn is a portion of the time of God's purpose. At any one moment, the purpose of God may not be fully understood, as in the case of Job or Habakkuk. Yet the answer will surely come; and meanwhile 'the right-eous shall live by his faithfulness' (Hab. 2.4; Rom. 1.17), which means that he shall live in obedience to the divine election while certain of the divine reliability and of the divine promises. The elect may even be forced to assume the role of a suffering servant, bearing in his body the wounds of a fallen humanity, yet in the hope and trust that his suffering is not in vain because he is simply following his Lord.

The all-embracing guide to relative choices and ethical judgments is, of course, the law of neighbourly love. This means that the first and primary consideration behind all endeavour is the righteousness of God which impels a deep concern for the neighbour. Quietism is an extreme form of individualism; but if one loves his neighbour as himself, then he cannot stand by quietly when his neighbour is not receiving the justice one expects or obtains for himself. The law of love presumes the social context of existence, and it can never be repeated too often that in the Bible this love is to express itself in a vital concern for justice. Much has been written in modern times to indicate the difference between, and the relation of, love and justice. Yet it must not be forgotten that the clear distinctions which we desire to make are not present in biblical thought or vocabulary. The biblical words for 'righteousness', 'justice' or 'judgment', and even 'vengeance', cannot be rendered adequately in another language precisely because in the major instances of theological usage they reflect the biblical knowledge of God's nature as the dominant Actor in history. Hence they involve both 'love' and 'justice'. These two conceptions simply cannot be separated because they are united in God. In whatever manner our sophistication leads us to describe the relation between the two, it must not be forgotten that in the Bible the social context of neighbourly love involves a passionate concern for justice, a concern which in the cross of Christ leads the elect to proclaim to the world the righteousness of God against all unrighteousness. God's election impels one to take part in the struggle for justice, to attack all misuse of power and of earthly goods of which men are stewards, and to challenge all forms of injustice, for in the end these are all types of rebellion and idolatry. While we normally think only of the Old Testament prophets in this connection, the dominant attitude of these men is vigorously espoused also by Jesus and by Paul, as was pointed out above in this chapter.

Is there any hope that the efforts of the elect can in any measure be successful in the world? The Bible gives no certain answer to this question. While numerous temporary successes can be indicated, the biblical community of faith is less interested in its own success than it is in God's. The destruction of Jerusalem and the cross of Christ indicated that present defeat is more to be expected than victory. Yet this did not deter a Jeremiah or a Peter from fulfilling his mission, because, while an earthly hope was crushed, the victory of God in the tragedy was observed and celebrated. It is this victory which gives the elect its hope of earth and which preserves an open future. That hope may not be fulfilled in our history, but it resists all attempts to make it otherworldly and unreal. It is the new earth, however altered, which 'shall be full of the knowledge of the Lord, as the waters cover the sea' (Isa. 11.9). It is in God's creation that every man shall sit 'under his vine and under his fig tree, and none shall make him afraid, for the mouth of the Lord of hosts hath spoken it' (Mic. 4.4). And this is 'because the creation itself will be set free from its bondage to decay and obtain the glorious liberty of the people of God' (Rom. 8.21).

INDEX OF BIBLICAL
REFERENCES

171

173

INDEX OF SUBJECTS

175